THANKS, PG!

by

John Isaac Jones

A Novel

Copyright © 2014 by John Isaac Jones

All rights are reserved. No part of this book may be used or reproduced in any manner whatsoever without written permission, except in the case of brief quotations embodied in critical articles or reviews.

Dedicated

to

Generoso Pope Jr.

Preface

When I was in my twenties, if you asked me who had had the most influence on my life, I would have said Bob Dylan, the great minstrel who plumbed the heart and soul of the sixties and seventies with his songs. If you had asked me when I was in my forties, I would have said Carlos Castaneda, the great anthropologist who, as a student of the mythical Mexican shaman Don Juan, tried to teach other human beings how to expand their perceptual abilities. Now that I am in my late sixties, I realize that the single person who influenced my life more than any other was an Italian man from New York named Generoso Pope Jr., commonly known as 'GP.'

From my earliest days, I knew that I was destined to be a reporter. After years as a young journalist in the Deep South, however, I feared the subjects I was destined to write about would be forever confined to city council meetings, automobile accidents, murder trials, tornadoes, board of education feuds and biggest pumpkin contests.

In my heart, I yearned for more. I dreamed of traveling the world, making scads of money and covering the wildest, craziest stories the world had to offer. Thanks to that little Italian man, those dreams would come true beyond my wildest dreams. This book was written to honor him.

This book is a work of autobiographical fiction. In short, I took the facts of my life and wrote it as a novel. While most of the stories contained herein are true, in some instances, I changed the facts of some incidents and exaggerated the details of others in order to come up with a more interesting, entertaining book.

I changed Mr. Pope's name because, in reality, the man was so much larger than life that the constraints of hum-drum reality could not do justice to the wonderful madness of the man. If I had used Mr. Pope's true name, then, in readers' minds, they would have pictured Mr. Pope throughout the book.

I changed my name because I didn't want the work to sound like just one more boring book about a retired journalist who recites his life experiences over and over to the refrains of "I did this. I did that. I went here. I went there etc."

While I have used the real names of people in most cases, in some instances, the names of the actual persons, especially with regard to Hollywood celebrities, were changed to protect against lawsuits.

Finally, I tried to create a work which would not only be a record of my life experiences, but keep the reader engaged until the final page.

John I. Jones

Table of Contents

Chapter 1 1
Chapter 2 12
Chapter 3 21
Chapter 4 35
Chapter 5 48
Chapter 6 58
Chapter 7 71
Chapter 8 83
Chapter 9 95
Chapter 10 105
Chapter 11 115
Chapter 12 129
Chapter 13 146
Chapter 14 159
Chapter 15 171
Chapter 16 186
Chapter 17 196
Chapter 18 211

Thanks, PG!

Chapter 1

In the Beginning

We are all born with a predetermined destiny. Unfortunately, many people are never quite capable of identifying their life purpose and end up accepting only what fickle fate decides to provide them. Then there are those who successfully identify their purpose and spend their entire lives trying to achieve those goals, only to fail miserably. Finally, there are the lucky ones who not only identify their assigned destiny, but achieve it beyond their wildest dreams. I was one of the lucky ones. This is my story.

*****

In southwest Tennessee, the mighty Tennessee River struts strong and blue due southward through the Appalachian foothills to Chattanooga, then turns eastward and winds into the heart of North Central Alabama past Huntsville, Decatur, and finally, Guntersville, where its tributaries fan out into a smaller web of rivers with Indian names like Etowah, Tomoka, and Okaloosa. One of these tributaries, the Coosa, then snakes its way southward into Jackson County, Alabama, where it makes a sharp bend near the town of Hamilton. There, directly at the bend, rests a white, six-story structure called the Holy Name of Jesus Hospital. It was in that hospital, on the banks of the Coosa River, that I was born William Donald Johnson on National Newspaper Reporters Day, April 20, 1942.

My mother later recalled that, as the attending physician slapped my lily-white behind, she heard over the radio piped in to the delivery room that newspaper editors and reporters were celebrating in New York.

My earliest memories of life were looking into my mother's eyes. In my mother's face, I could see the sun, the moon, and the stars. Here, I always sensed peace and tranquility and, when she smiled, I saw the warm glow of the rising sun. If I was sick, hurt, or in trouble, I always knew that I could count on my mother. In later years, even if I was in the wrong, my mother was always there to support me. I couldn't have asked for a more devoted, loving mother. I truly believe that my mother's nursing profession strengthened her sense of motherhood.

The first few years of my life were spent on a farm. I remember being dragged by a calf when I was three, maybe four years old. My father had a young calf grazing in a field behind our house. He told me to go out and move the calf to another area where there was fresher, green grass. As soon as I had the calf untied, it launched into a full run and dragged me more than a hundred yards across the grassy field. When I finally released the rope, I was a crying, helpless clump of scratches and bruises.

When my parents saw what had happened, they came racing to my rescue.

"He's bleeding," my mother said urgently, noting the small cuts on my face and forehead. "I've got to get him inside."

Instantly, she swept me up in her arms and took me into the kitchen, where she carefully cleaned and dressed my wounds.

"He's not hurt," my father said solemnly. "Just a few little scratches and bruises. Those will make a man out of him."

When I was four, my father bought a big blackboard that had all of the numbers and letters stamped along the top. I

Thanks, PG!

would spend countless hours writing and spelling words on that blackboard. Nothing pleased me more than finding long words like "encyclopedia" and "geography" and spelling them over and over on the blackboard until I mastered them. The king of all long words was "antidisestablishmentarianism." I didn't know what it meant when I was four, but I could spell it, and it was the longest word I knew at the time. Soon, I could read the comic strips in the local newspapers. I knew "Dagwood and Blondie" was one of my father's favorites, and the moment the newspaper arrived, I would read it and be prepared to discuss it with my father that night at the dinner table.

From my earliest days, I felt there was nothing more beautiful than books, those little repositories of information that contained all the knowledge mankind had amassed through the ages. I remember collecting books and magazines and making a crude bookcase out of three pieces of wood. I placed my books inside and admired the beauty of all that knowledge within those little slats of thin wood.

For me, the printed word was the equivalent of happiness. I remember one day being at a neighbor's house and rummaging through an old barn, where we found boxes upon boxes of old comic books. I looked down at the boxes of neatly stacked Lash Larue and Gene Autry comic books and I felt my heart soar with gladness at all the happiness contained therein.

Although my name was William Donald, my mother told everyone in the family that she wanted me to be called "Billy."

"I don't want him to be called 'Bill,'" she said. "That's too plain and it reminds people of a bird's beak. 'Billy' has a soft sound and it's easy to remember."

"Call that child 'Billy Don,'" my grandmother countered. "Boys named Billy are a dime a dozen."

During the early years, my mother always referred to me as "Billy," but as the years rolled past, my grandmother, my father, and my cousins called me "Billy Don" and, by the time I was five or six, my mother relented and the entire world referred to me as "Billy Don."

In elementary school, I was a good student, but I was always in trouble. In the second grade, I only missed two spelling words the entire year. I spelled the word "white" as "wite" and the word "coming" as "comeing."

My teacher, Mrs. Sarah Williams, caught me trying to sneak a Roy Rogers comic book that was hidden inside my coloring book into class.

"Billy Don, this is nothing more than trash," she said, holding the Roy Rogers comic book up for all the class to see. "All it will do is lead you to a life of crime."

She gave me ten licks with a paddle and threw the comic book into the fires of the coal stove the classroom used for heat.

Early on, my father taught me a strong work ethic. He always said the greatest pleasure life had to offer was work and, if a job was worth doing, it was worth doing right. In the wintertime, when I turned six, my father announced my single chore was to bring in the coal and kindling every night for the morning fire. My father always got up early and built the fire in the coal heater. One afternoon, I came in from school, played all afternoon with my cousin, and failed to bring in the coal and kindling. My father woke me at 5:30 a.m. and made me go out into the morning cold and gather the coal and kindling. I was crying and angry at the time, but I learned my lesson. It never happened again!

When I was quite young, one of the main topics of conversation at family gatherings was deciding what profession I should follow as an adult. My mother had dreams of me becoming a doctor.

Thanks, PG!

"Doctors make lots of money," she said. "And because they save lives, they're well-respected in the community."

"No, I want Billy Don to become a preacher," said my deeply religious grandmother. "I think he would make a fine preacher to spread the word of God."

When I was only seven or eight, she would dress me in a suit and tie and take me to the Old Harmony Baptist Church in Hamilton on Sundays. Before we entered the church, she would do a crosscheck: straight tie, hair neatly combed, Bible in my left hand so my right would be free to shake hands. She pointed out the pastor and deacons and explained that each had "the look of the Lord." She said I should learn to develop that special look because it was the foundation of becoming a "fine preacher."

Meanwhile, in my heart of hearts, I had a totally different profession in mind, although I dared not mention it to my mother or grandmother. I wanted to be a reporter, a person who attended major world events and wrote about them in newspapers and magazines. I had read books and seen movies about reporters, and I couldn't imagine a single profession that would be more exciting and rewarding. I felt a person could make a difference as a reporter. He could expose corruption, get a front row seat to the world's disasters, and meet the most powerful people on earth. A reporter could stand up for all the things that decent-minded people held near and dear... truth, justice, and the American way.

When I turned ten, my father briefly owned a barbecue restaurant in a Hamilton suburb called Glencoe. "The Pig" was a little roadside affair where couples and single men could go to eat barbecue, drink some beers, and meet members of the opposite sex. There was a Wurlitzer jukebox, a dance floor, and rooms out back. It was my first introduction to "sin," as my grandmother put it.

"Whores and whore-mongers are all that go into a place like that," she proclaimed when my mother announced that my father was opening the business.

On Saturday nights, I loved watching the free-spirited lifestyle of the restaurant's patrons. I sang along with the popular hits of the day like "The Wayward Wind," "Put Another Nickel In," and "Bonaparte's Retreat." As I watched the men kissing and fondling the women in the booths, I yearned to be an adult and be wild and free around women.

*****

In keeping with my love of words, I naturally migrated to the printed page. When I was thirteen, I answered an ad in a comic book that sought young boys to sell a small newspaper called *The Grit*. Published in Williamsport, Pennsylvania, it was a tabloid-sized weekly newspaper that had national news, human-interest stories, puzzles, comics, and an overall inspirational "feel-good" spirit. Once I was signed on, I would receive the new edition, read it thoroughly upon arrival, and point out to prospective customers my favorite stories.

Over some four months, sometimes bicycling six miles from my home, I built a route of twenty-eight customers. With each new edition, *Grit* publishers promised huge rewards to delivery agents who could enlarge their routes. One day at school, DeWayne Vaughn, a fellow student at Hamilton Junior High, said he was abandoning his *Grit* route of thirty-two customers because his family was moving. I told him I wanted to assume his route. After adding DeWayne's route, I had a grand total of seventy-two customers. One day, when I got off the school bus, I saw all of these packages stacked around the family mailbox. There was a baseball bat, two gloves, a watch, a New York Yankees jacket, a kaleidoscope, a replica of a Colt revolver, and many more gifts the publisher had sent

Thanks, PG!

because I had gained new customers. It was a solid lesson for me that hard work pays off.

*****

The next stop in my print destiny would take me to the Hamilton Motor Inn, the largest, ritziest hotel in Hamilton, where I got a job printing menus. From the first moment I saw that little hand-cranked press, I thought I was Gutenberg. The type was built by gathering individual letters on a spindle, then feeding them into grooves on the face of the press. Black ink was applied to the roller with a spatula, and I always had to run some test passes to be sure the ink was uniform across the type. There were never enough E's and U's, and the kitchen manager was too cheap to buy more.

"Just do the best you can," he would say.

Since the letter E is the most frequently used vowel, I guarded and hoarded them as if they were gold. I dreaded seeing the word "vegetable" on the menu because there were three E's. Once, I was faced with spelling the word "frankfurters" at a time when I had no U's, but I had plenty of A's. I ended up spelling the word "frankfarters" and sent out the menus with that spelling. No one ever said anything.

In April of 1957, a month before I was to graduate from Hamilton Junior High, I and the other thirty-six students made our class trip to the state capital in Montgomery, Alabama. The objective was to tour the capital landmarks, gain some knowledge as to how state government worked, and visit the governor's mansion. At the time, the state's governor was one "Big Jim" Folsom, a colorful giant of a man famous for wearing red suspenders and drinking a fifth of scotch a day. After we had toured the state legislature and listened to a boring, drawn-out explanation of how bills make it through the house and senate, we arrived at the governor's mansion.

Once the bus was parked, the school principal went inside and reappeared some twenty minutes later with the announcement that the governor would be out momentarily to greet us from the mansion's veranda. Moments later, the governor appeared and waved to us. As usual, he was wearing his trademark red suspenders and, as he was famous for, snapped the suspenders with his thumbs against his huge whiskey belly to the delight of the junior high students. Accompanying the governor was his sister "Big Ruby" and her daughter Cornelia, who, at the tender age of thirteen, was already a stunning beauty. On that day, as I sat in the bus with my fellow students and waved to the governor, his sister, and his niece, I never dreamed that, twenty years later, I would know the most intimate details of little Cornelia's sex life.

When I was in high school, my mother was adamant that I should start making plans to become a physician, but I explained that I had neither the patience to spend ten years in school and she and my father didn't have the money to pay the tuition. She agreed, but she said she wanted me to stay in the medical field. As a result, to please my mother, I decided to become a pharmacist. In May of 1959, when I entered the eleventh grade at Hamilton High, I signed up for the work-study program.

In the program, I would work in the pharmacy at the local Baptist hospital for four hours in the morning, then attend my classes in the afternoon. The chief pharmacist was a deeply religious, well-meaning man who had always wanted a son. At the hospital, my job was to deliver filled prescriptions for patients to the nursing stations. When not making deliveries, I would perform menial chores in the pharmacy like preparing liquid soap, typing labels for prescriptions, and maintaining stock room records. The job was fun and paid fifty cents an hour.

Thanks, PG!

In late May of 1960, I graduated from Hamilton High School. As I walked across the auditorium stage to receive my diploma, I wondered what my future had in store. I looked around me and saw my fellow students preparing for college, getting married and settling down, and starting low-paying jobs. I didn't know what my future held, but I knew I certainly wasn't going to follow the lives I saw around me.

*****

In keeping with my mother's wishes, I enrolled in the pre-pharmacy curriculum at a small community college. As in high school, I was a good student, and I dug into the disciplines of organic chemistry, biology, physics, and math. Over the next two years, I became well versed in molecular structures, human anatomy, and the scientific nomenclature necessary to identify the various forms of life. All the while I was attending classes, I was still working at the Baptist hospital. In the fall of 1962, I enrolled in the Pharmacy School at Auburn University. Upon enrollment, the chief pharmacist had arranged for the hospital to pay for my tuition and board with the stipulation that, upon graduation, I would return and work for the hospital for at least five years.

At Auburn University, I realized quickly that I was about to achieve a goal that, in my heart of hearts, I really didn't want. I knew I could never spend my lifetime counting pills out of a big bottle and putting them into a labeled smaller bottle. I had veered far away from my assigned destiny. On the other hand, I didn't know how to tell the people who had believed in and supported me that I wanted out.

I knew I had to be true to myself and do what I wanted, not what others expected of me. This meant I had to crush the dreams of my mother, my father, and the chief pharmacist at the hospital. I felt that the world was too big and too rich and too interesting for me to spend my life in such a confined, routine, humdrum environment. I knew that my life was destined to be spent around words, not pills. In my heart, I knew that my destiny lay with letters, words, sentences, and paragraphs. In clear, precise language, fate had commanded me to go forth and write.

I stopped attending pharmacy classes and started spending all day in the university library. I would spend eight to ten hours a day reading anything and everything. I started with Homer, Aristotle, Plato, Nietzsche, and Freud. I read most of Hugo, Kafka, Hemingway, Dickens, and Faulkner. The love of poetry I discovered in high school exploded full bore during that period, and I read Byron, Keats, Shelly, Coleridge, and Matthew Arnold. I memorized famous poems such as Dylan Thomas's "Do Not Go Gentle into That Good Night" and "Fern Hill," and I spent endless hours reading Poe, Longfellow, Gerard Manley Hopkins, Emily Dickinson, and the sonnets of Shakespeare. I dreamed of visiting the lake district of England and seeing the homes of the famous poets. I yearned to travel to Stratford and see where Shakespeare walked and talked, but, in my heart, I felt it would never come to pass.

One day, after I stopped attending class, I went to see a movie entitled *Five Weeks in a Balloon*. Based on a Jules Verne novel, it was the story of a professor and his minions traveling around the world in a hot-air balloon. One of the characters was a tall, slim, well-endowed Italian woman whom the credits listed as Francesca Monterrey. As I watched her flit about in her dark, sultry sexuality, I knew I was in love.

While walking back to my dorm room after the movie, I remember thinking, *I would give anything on this earth to know a beautiful woman like that*. Little did I know that seventeen years later, she would become one of my closest friends.

Thanks, PG!

By the end of the semester, I had failed all of my pharmacy classes and returned to Hamilton to face the music. The chief pharmacist told me I couldn't work at the hospital any longer and I would have to pay back the money the hospital had paid for my tuition and board. My mother cried. My father shook his head and said nothing. I was delirious with delight. It was the first time in my life that I, and I alone, had decided what I wanted to do with my life.

*****

Over the next four years, I wandered aimlessly. I worked several different jobs, including racking balls at the Stag, working for the state highway department, and doing day labor with a concrete construction company. I wandered out to California for eight months. To survive, I passed out samples door to door, worked at a service station, and had various delivery jobs. California had introduced me to two things: Bob Dylan and weed. Both would be mainstays later in my life. I wandered down to New Orleans for several months, where I sold popcorn and cotton candy during Mardi Gras, worked as a sander at an auto body shop, and finally a painter during renovation of an old hotel. I was a rudderless ship going nowhere in particular.

During those wandering years, I knew that my love of words and writing superseded everything else I could ever want to do, but I was clueless as to how to find my path. Finally, I started researching the lives of famous writers and journalists, trying to discover some common path that led them to a lifetime of writing. The common denominator I found was that virtually all of them had been either newspaper or magazine reporters at some point in their lives. I thought perhaps if I could get a toe in the door at some newspaper, I would end up with a job as a reporter. I had a plan.

11

Chapter 2

Ink in My Blood

My plan started to take shape in early May of 1968 while I was working at the Stag pool hall. For some time, I had known Chris Whitehead, a regular who was employed at the local newspaper, the *Hamilton Courier*. On several occasions, while we were playing eight ball, I had asked Chris how to get a job as a reporter at the *Courier*, and he always replied that I should talk to Paul Malone, the executive editor. I felt that since I had no training and no experience, it would be a useless exercise, so I had dismissed Chris's suggestions. One afternoon, Chris mentioned off-handedly that there was an opening in his department and, if I was interested, I should reply to the classified ad in that day's edition. Somehow, my instincts told me this was my opportunity.

The following morning, I answered the ad and was instructed to be present for an interview two days later. The director of advertising was a short, gray-haired man named Randall, who, from the looks of the puffiness around his eyes, was overworked and underpaid, and he made short shrift of the interview.

"Do you have a driver's license?" he asked.

"Yes, sir!" I replied.

"Are you bondable?"

I replied in the affirmative again.

"Report for work on Monday!"

Thanks, PG!

It was the shortest job interview I had ever had in my life.

"Dispatch," as it was commonly called, was part of the newspaper's advertising department, and back in the days before digital printing, this department was responsible for delivering the ad proofs to the client for approval.

So, for seven months, I traversed the hills and valleys of Jackson County delivering advertising proofs. My biggest personal gain from working in Dispatch, after overseeing the production of ads day after day, was gaining an intimate understanding of how the entire publication was produced each and every day. Essentially, Dispatch taught me the daily mechanics of newspaper production.

In January of 1969, my plan took a giant leap forward. One day, the production schedule was almost two hours past the normal press time. I asked a composing room employee what the problem was and he explained that production was behind because the person who regularly prepared the newswire tape for the editorial department had suddenly quit. Immediately, a light went on in my head. I went straight to the newsroom and spoke with Arthur Ray Shaw, another long-time friend from the Stag who was the city editor.

"I heard you have a new job opening in the wire room," I said.

"You have to get up at four every morning to be at work on time," he said. "That's why we can't keep anybody."

He explained that the production system was based on all newswire tape being ready when the day editor came on at six a.m. If newswire tape wasn't ready, the day editor had to match tape to the appropriate stories himself, which threw the production schedule behind.

"I'll make you a good man if you'll give me a shot," I said.

"You need to talk to Paul," he replied.

That afternoon, I spoke with Paul Malone, the executive editor. I explained my ambition to be a reporter and my interest in the tape-rolling job. After a discussion of salary and small talk, he took me into the wire room and showed me what the job entailed. Each news story that came off the wire services had an accompanying perforated tape, which, when inserted into the typesetting machine, would automatically set the type for the accompanying text. In short, each newswire story had to be matched to its corresponding tape. He gave me a key and instructed me to report to work the next morning.

Now I got a first-hand look at newspaper production from the editorial side. I would arrive at work every morning at five a.m. and start rolling wire tape. By six a.m., I'd be finished and the production editor, a short, grizzled older man, would arrive to start filling in the pages.

From the moment he started work, I watched closely as he sorted out the stories. Potential front-page stories went into one stack, Page 2 stories another, and features for the inside leadoff pages went into still another pile. Once he started filling up the paper, I would stand over his shoulder and watch him write headlines. Of course, I understood fonts and counts from working in the advertising department, and I would offer suggestions to help him create a headline that would have a stronger impact. If he disagreed with my suggestions, I remained quiet and humble. Immediately, I could see that my vocabulary and felicity for words was much greater than that of an editor who had been on the job for twenty-five years.

When not acting as go-for, I had menial writing chores. One of my responsibilities was to call the local airport, get projected temperatures, and write the day's weather. Once that was done, around ten a.m., the funeral home reps would arrive with the day's obituaries and I was expected to edit those. I would write civic club announcements, brief listings of the recent Eagle Scouts, and occasionally a caption for a photo. The front page proof would come out at noon and, after it was proofed and corrected, I would spend the afternoon answering

14

Thanks, PG!

the phone. I was diligent and thorough in my efforts, and I could see that the executive editor was happy with me.

After some three months, I was assigned my first story. A small town outside of Hamilton had bought a new fire truck and my job was to interview the mayor and fire chief about their new hardware. Once it had been written and filed, I followed the one-page story through the entire print process. Immediately, after the type was set, I went to the composing room to see the galley. When the proof came out of composing, I personally read it for typos and put my okay on it for printing.

The following week, I was assigned to write a weekly column called "Centennial Corner," about the history of Jackson County, which was celebrating its centennial year. Every fall, the sports editor would assign me to cover high school and sometimes college football games. I received ten dollars for covering the game and writing the story. I also received a five-dollar meal allowance and gas mileage to and from games. I thought I had died and gone to heaven.

I was on my way. It was during this period that I learned the basics of constructing stories in every news category. "Straight up" stories, as editors called them, were "just the facts" stories. These were bare bones, no-frills stories that were reported with nothing more than the who, what, when, where, and how of a news event. If the story was a feature, these were invariably human-interest stories where I could take some poetic license, exaggerate a bit, and push a quote to make it stronger or more colorful for impact. Sports stories, on the other hand, allowed even further poetic freedoms since sports was naturally an event that lent itself to colorful excitement, high emotions, and a sense of the spectacular.

After two years, I was assigned a county courthouse beat. This was primarily the sheriff's office, which focused on the current and past apprehension of criminals. Also, there was an occasional murder trial, announcements from the local health department, and a smattering of stories, mostly features, from the county extension agriculture office and the county tax office.

*****

Some of my happiest days at the *Courier* were covering murder trials. Early on, I learned how to synopsize testimony, understand attorneys' motions, and develop a sixth sense about juries. At the time, I never dreamed these days would be basic training for my involvement twenty-four years later covering the "trial of the century."

During that period, I made every effort to pick the minds of fellow reporters for tips on becoming a better journalist. One of those was Reuben Killebrew. Originally from Clarksville, Tennessee, Reuben, who was in his sixties, had spent his entire life around newspapers.

"You can't write something until you know what you want to write," he said.

That was such a simple, important concept of writing, but I had not fully grasped it until Reuben said it in so many words.

From Arthur Ray, I learned what a good editor can do. The act of writing is essentially putting words on paper and, as creator, the writer will invariably produce more words than necessary or, in the heat of creativity, produce copy that isn't always clear. That's where a competent editor can make an aspiring journalist a better reporter. At times, I hated him for forcing me to write and rewrite passages until they were clear, but in the end, it paid off. Arthur Ray was my drill sergeant.

Finally, there was Virginia Block, the paper's state editor. From her, I learned the basics of investigations, the most complex, intense form of newspaper reporting. A short, masculine-acting woman in her early fifties, she was a chain

Thanks, PG!

smoker and fearless as an investigative reporter. Jackson County, like most Alabama Counties, was rife with political corruption, and Virginia dug up bombshell stories, but the front office often refused to publish them.

Through her sources in Montgomery, she had uncovered a story that William Hixon, the county's most powerful politician and owner of a big-rig trucking company in town, had obtained sixteen truck tags for his company's trucks without paying a dime. A regular John Q. Citizen would have paid $216,750 for the tags, but through the good-old-boy system in the state capital, he had paid nothing. Virginia had meticulously gathered all of her evidence, public records, tapes of interviews, and photos, and presented the story to the executive editor. It was a bombshell, and the executive editor passed it to the publisher's son for approval.

"It's just politics!" the publisher's son said. "These things never change and we'll accomplish nothing by publishing this story."

The story died as a result of the publisher's son protecting the status quo. I felt so sorry for Virginia. I had watched how carefully and methodically she had put the story together. Every word was backed up with solid proof, and the story was written in a lean, brisk narrative style that strong investigative pieces require. Now all of her hard work was for nothing, but I had learned so much about investigations by watching and listening to Virginia. It would pay off handsomely in later years.

It wasn't the first time *Courier* publishers had manipulated the news. The previous year, while working in Dispatch, I had heard stories of the front office squelching stories about their friends who had been arrested for marijuana possession. Similar stories about non-friends of the publishers were printed without question.

After five years, I had become a seasoned news veteran at the *Courier*. My knack for words had reached a truly expert level. I had learned the intricacies of local politics at both the city and county level. I had covered the county courthouse beat for two years and had even pinch-hit for the city hall reporter when he was sick or on vacation. I could write hard news, features, sports, shoot photo spreads, oversee daily production from start to finish, and had an excellent understanding of how to conduct investigations. Also, I learned "desk work," the ability to gather, organize, and assimilate all of the day's content —reporters' and wire stories as well as syndicated material—into a single edition. This included writing headlines for each story and arranging the stories and text on the pages in such a way that the reader's eye moved naturally across the page. In terms of my journalistic training, learning "desk work" was the icing on the cake.

One afternoon in late November of 1972, the publisher's son called me in. I had been the production editor on the previous Sunday edition and had run a banner headline about an impending strike at the town's steel mill. He said the *Courier* couldn't afford to run such stories during the holiday season because people would stop spending money for Christmas and the paper's advertisers needed the money.

"If our advertisers don't make money, we don't make money," he said.

I replied that I felt my job was to report the news, not manage it. Maybe I was asking for it, I'm not sure, but that was my response. I had already lost all respect for him over the William Hixon story.

"Close the door," he said ominously.

I knew that was the signal I was about to get my butt reamed. I closed the door.

After the chewing-out was complete, he had some choice words for his closing.

Thanks, PG!

"Now drag your bleeding ass back to the newsroom and see if you can follow instructions."

When I walked back down the hallway to the newsroom, I knew I was gone from the *Courier*. I didn't know how long it would take, but I knew I was gone.

Three weeks later, I was in Birmingham to cover the Iron Bowl. This football event was the annual rivalry between Alabama and Auburn, the state's premier college football teams. The sports editor had asked me to work the sidelines for color and photographs. During the game, I met Jim Bostick, the long-time photographer for the *Birmingham Age-Herald* whom I had befriended at various sporting events over the years. As we followed the teams up and down the sidelines, we snapped photos and chatted.

"The *Age-Herald* is expanding the news staff this next spring," he said. "They're extending the retail coverage from Birmingham proper to the outlying counties and are going to create a metro staff."

"Oh, really?" I replied innocently.

"Yeah," Jim continued. "They're going to be hiring at least three more reporters."

The following Monday morning, I went straight to Arthur Ray and asked him who did the hiring at the *Age-Herald*.

"Bill Jacobsen," he replied. "He's the assistant managing editor."

Immediately, I called the *Age-Herald*, finally got through to the assistant managing editor, and told him I was interested in a job on the new metro staff. After I held my breath for a moment, he said to send him a resume. The following January, I went to Birmingham for the interview. Bill Jacobsen, a chubby, bespectacled man in his late thirties, was an ambitious, no-nonsense go-getter who had a master's degree in journalism.

"We want hard-hitting stories which represent truth, justice, and the highest traditions of American journalism," he said.

"We're looking for in-depth investigative pieces that earn respect for our publication and shake up the status quo."

I told him those were the types of stories I wanted to do. Finally, when I left the interview and was driving back to Hamilton, I was flush with excitement about getting the job. Five weeks passed, then, out of the blue, I got a call from Jacobsen.

"We want you to come to work for us," he said calmly.

I was so excited that my heart skipped a beat. Four days later, I was more than happy to present my resignation to the publisher's son.

Thanks, PG!

Chapter 3

Investigative Reporter

The Birmingham *Age-Herald* was the largest daily newspaper in Alabama. They were a full-blown metropolitan daily and had editors I had never dreamed of. There was a religion editor, a book editor, a movie editor, and even a music critic. I never dreamed I would work for a paper with a music critic. Around the rim of the copy desk were seven editors who read the same story for content, spelling, punctuation, clarity, and potential libel. Also, for the first time, I had access to a research department that had clips of all previous stories on a given subject readily available. They even had company cars, which reporters could sign out for long trips. These people were dead serious about reporting the news.

The metro editor was Charles Bayliss, a young, dark-haired man from Huntsville who had spent four years as a reporter with the *Mobile Press-Register*. He was an affable, easy-going editor and had a simple, fluid writing style that I much admired. The Metro beat was divided into three parts. I was assigned the area south of Birmingham, which included the cities of Bessemer, Midfield, and Fairfield. I had never had so much physical space—forty square miles—on a beat before, so I meticulously analyzed how to best handle the coverage. I knew that my priorities were the three major cities, especially Bessemer, and I decided to focus my primary efforts there.

As I drove to Bessemer on my first day, I was reminded that this was the childhood home of my father. Although my father had passed, I longed to excel in Bessemer if for no other reason than to honor his memory. Just south of downtown Bessemer was a little park with a bronze statue of a World War I soldier. As a child, when we would visit my father's relatives in Bessemer, we would always drive past the park and my father would say "Doughboy." Every day, when I arrived in Bessemer, I would park my car at "Doughboy" Park and walk the two blocks to city hall. The park was a sentimental point of reference for me and provided a sense of security and familiarity to which I could relate.

I spent the first few months taking potential sources to lunch, learning who had access to what information, identifying sources of public information, and generally learning the lay of the political land.

As my list of sources grew, it wasn't long before allegations of political corruption started to surface. From the beginning, I knew that to make a name for myself, I would have to do investigative stories. Any reporter fresh out of journalism school could write "straight-up" news, but this type of investigative reporting required a discipline that eluded even some of the most veteran reporters. Now my experiences with Virginia Block started to pay off.

In Bessemer, Tom Ashburn had been the Commissioner of Public Works for sixteen years. A chubby, baby-faced man in his early sixties, Tom always appeared cordial and made it a point to befriend the press at city council meetings. Some twenty years earlier, he had incorporated a company in town called Ashco. County incorporation records listed Ashco as a company that provided landscaping, excavation, and rubbish removal services. Incorporation records had been signed by him and the company address was a local P.O. Box. The problem was, according to sources, the company's employees

Thanks, PG!

were on the payroll of the City Public Works Department, and all of Ashco's equipment was owned by the city.

I started to monitor the sites where city equipment was performing work each day. Every morning, I would go to the city's equipment storage lot and follow employees and city equipment to the day's job. For over a week, I followed city employees to various jobs. There was a gas line extension, rubbish removal at a state park, and a water main leak at the police department. All were performed on public property. I did notice one thing. None of the city's equipment was designated as city-owned. I thought that was strange.

I got a break. The following Monday morning, after I parked at "Doughboy" Park and headed to the city council meeting, I was approached by a smallish, sunburned man in his late forties who introduced himself only as Earl.

"I've seen you at the reporter's table during city council meetings," he said, "but I didn't want to approach you in public."

Earl said he had been a bulldozer operator with the city for many years and was recently dismissed after a dispute with his foreman. Earl knew the story I was working on and told me I should talk to Waylon Livingston, a construction firm owner in south Bessemer.

"He's got everything you need," Earl said as he quickly disappeared down the street.

That afternoon, I found Waylon Livingston Construction in the phone book and set up a meeting with the owner the following morning. Waylon said his company had built a huge apartment complex called Covington Green in south Bessemer some four years earlier and Ashburn's company had done most of the landscaping and excavation services.

"When the job was finished, I wrote him a check for almost $14,000. I never asked about who was doing the work."

"Do you still have the check?" I asked.

"We'll see," he replied.

That afternoon, he took me to a storage locker and we started digging through old company documents. Finally, after two hours, we found the check.

From the moment I presented Commissioner Ashburn with my findings, both of us knew he had been caught red-handed. Even worse, it was all on paper.

"I thought you were my friend," he said innocently.

"I am your friend," I replied. "But you can't be collecting money for excavation work that was performed with city equipment and employees."

He denied that the work had been done by city employees and tried to defend himself with lies, but I knew, and he knew, it was all to no avail. The following Sunday, the *Age-Herald* carried the story with a banner headline and photos of the check. Ashburn resigned three weeks later.

*****

After the Ashburn story, I got a reputation as an investigator. Suddenly, investigations started coming at me from all directions. There was a state health department employee who claimed several drugstore chains had been over-billing the state for services. There was the case of the civil rights worker in Fairfield who had received a two-million-dollar HUD grant for a low-income apartment project but, after six months, the money had disappeared and no work had been done. A former mayor of one west Birmingham municipality claimed that a current council member was receiving a $50,000 a year kickback after winning a multi-million-dollar contract for a major highway-paving firm. Alabama was pure heaven for investigative reporters because corruption was rampant.

Thanks, PG!

In the late summer of 1974, I was assigned an investigation by the front office. The managing editor at the *Age-Herald* was a man named John Bloomfield. Bloomfield, known for years as a crusading journalist, had been part of the team that had cleaned up Phenix City in the fifties. Another member of the team was Conrad Tyler, who had since left south Alabama and was currently probate judge of nearby Sheffield County. These two men had the power, the contacts, and the will to tackle corruption at its core.

I had known for some time that Judge Tyler and long-time Sheffield County Sheriff Charles Walton were mortal political enemies. Once, at a civic club meeting in Birmingham, I had heard Tyler ranting about how the sheriff "wore two hats" in the county. The judge charged that, as sheriff, he not only had law enforcement power, but through long-standing political appointments, he also had prosecutorial power in the district attorney's office. Tyler said Sheriff Walton had absolute power on both sides of the law in Sheffield County. At the time I heard Tyler speak, it had no current relevance, so I dismissed the judge's ranting.

In late July of 1974, Bloomfield called me and fellow metro beat reporter Ron Jacobs into his office. He said he wanted a thorough investigation of Sheriff Walton, and he wanted a story before the upcoming election. The sheriff's opponent in the upcoming election was Sheffield County Coroner Bill Jenkins.

"There is no end to the evil this man in capable of," Bloomfield said, "so I want the two of you to be together all of the time you're in Sheffield County."

Ron, a mustachioed, forever-smiling bear of a young man was a native of Midfield and a recent graduate of the University of Alabama Journalism School. He'd been editor of the university newspaper and a member of the prestigious

Sigma Delta Chi. Early on, he told me his life's ambition was to win a Pulitzer.

The following Monday, Ron and I turned our energies to the managing editor's assignment. Once we started talking to sources, we realized Bloomfield was right. There was no end to the evil of this man. He owed gambling debts in Las Vegas. He was protecting fugitives. His minions were selling confiscated drugs to jail inmates. He was receiving kickbacks from several local companies that did business with the sheriff's office. This man was a classic example of a corrupt southern sheriff.

As a public figure, Sheriff Walton was straight out of the movies. He drove around town in a gold-grilled Cadillac with eight-inch, solid-ivory cattle horns mounted prominently on the hood. During court appearances, he sported one-thousand-dollar alligator cowboy boots and smoked expensive Cuban cigars.

One of our contacts was a man named "Cowboy" Cochran, a local ne'er do well who had been in and out of the Sheffield County jail many times. He'd worked as a trustee in the jail kitchen.

"I've heard several times that the sheriff was getting kickbacks from the food distribution company which provides meals to prisoners," he said.

At one point, "Cowboy" also related an incident in which Sheriff Walton had transported a teenaged Native American girl from her jail cell to work as a "maid" at his vacation home at Waxahachie Creek and had his way with her. When "Cowboy" was relating that incident to me and Ron, I was absolutely shocked. That charge somehow went above and beyond mere political corruption.

Another source was a man named Austin Nails, a truck driver who had recently spent six months in the jail for writing

Thanks, PG!

bad checks. When we mentioned the incident about the Native American girl, he peered curiously at me.

"You need to talk to Jose Torres," he said. "The sheriff did the same thing to his daughter."

After the interview, I discussed it with Ron.

"We can't go chasing a sexual allegation like that," he said. "We would have to have an open-and-shut case to get it past Carlson," he added, referring to the newspaper's libel attorney.

"Let's talk to Jose Torres," I said.

"We'll go," Ron replied, "but we're wasting our time."

Jose Torres was a short, sunburned Mexican man who lived in a small Latino community on the outskirts of Smith's Station, the seat of Sheffield County. Hard working and illiterate, Jose spoke broken English and had been living hand-to-mouth all his life.

When Jose answered the door, we explained we were reporters investigating the local sheriff. Inside, we saw his wife, an obese, plain Mexican woman dressed in native garb, and a beautiful teenage daughter, maybe sixteen, who were cooking. Eyeing us suspiciously was a teenage son, maybe seventeen or eighteen, sitting on the front porch.

Once Jose learned what we wanted to discuss, he led us outside. The son followed. Out on the front porch, Jose introduced his son as Emilio and, speaking in broken English, said again and again the story about the sheriff taking his daughter to the vacation home wasn't true.

"Is lie! Is lie!" Jose repeated again and again. "No good! No good!"

After some thirty minutes of listening to "Is lie! Is lie!" Ron and I decided we were getting nowhere. We thanked him for his time and started to leave.

As we started back to our car, the son, who had been listening, called after us.

"No! No!" the father yelled when he saw his son was about to approach us.

The son angrily waved off his father and escorted us out to an oak tree in the front yard.

"My father is a coward," Emilio started. "If I could kill the sheriff myself, I would do it."

I could see the bitter hatred in his eyes.

Emilio said his family, who were fruit pickers, had passed through Sheffield County two years earlier en route to the tomato fields in central Alabama. After his father was stopped for a speeding violation, the officer noticed that the tag was expired and took the father to jail. Emilio said the family had no money to pay the six-hundred-dollar fine and court costs. Upon seeing his mother and his fourteen-year-old sister visiting Jose in jail, the sheriff visited the father in jail and told him they could "work something out." He suggested that, if the father could arrange for his daughter to clean his vacation home, he could arrange for the judge to show leniency. Emilio said the sheriff described the cleaning work as "community service."

"What could my father do?" Emilio said angrily, motioning with empty hands. "We have no money! What could he do?"

Emilio said the sheriff had his way with his sister during the five days she was at the vacation home.

After listening to Emilio's story, my blood boiled as we drove back to Birmingham.

"Even if it's true," Ron said, "they would never publish a story like that. That's something for the county justice system."

"Sheriff Walton is the justice system in Sheffield County," I said. "You know and I know nothing will ever be done."

Ron looked at me.

Thanks, PG!

"Bloomfield doesn't want a story about the sheriff having sex with some tomato picker's daughter," he replied. "He wants a story about corruption."

We rode quietly for several minutes.

"I know what you're thinking, Billy Don," Ron said, "but it's a waste of time. A story like that will never get into the paper."

Emilio's story had emboldened me to work harder than ever. I knew it would be a monumental task to uncover and prove point-by-point each and every allegation we had against the sheriff. I thought maybe, just maybe, we could prove enough to get him out of office in the upcoming election. At least that would be some justice for Jose's daughter.

We spent a month gathering allegations. One of our sources was a one-armed man named Albert Barker. A lifelong resident of Sheffield County and a close friend of the sheriff's opponent, Albert said we should talk to his cousin, Jimmy Barker. The cousin was a local Sheffield County thug who had killed two people. In one incident, Barker had been renting a house from an elderly man when they got into a rent dispute. In a drunken rage, Jimmy had gone to the man's house, pulled him out of bed, beat him unmercifully, ran over him with a car, and set him on fire. After a short trial, Jimmy had gotten off scot-free because of a technicality. In another instance, he had killed a man during a drunken argument over a woman and, after a short trial, won a verdict of self-defense. Albert said Jimmy knew the sheriff's "inner dealings" like nobody else.

A week before the election, we met with Jimmy Barker at Bill Jenkins' home in Smith's Station. From the first, I was suspicious of him. We asked about the sheriff giving confiscated weed to trusties to sell to inmates. We asked about kickbacks the sheriff was supposedly getting from the local automobile company that supplied cars for the sheriff's office.

We asked about his protecting fugitives. Again and again, he said he knew nothing. Finally, I asked him the blue-ribbon question.

"Is it true that he takes female inmates to his vacation home on the river under the guise of cleaning it and then has sex with them?"

He was stunned when I asked that question.

"I don't know anything about that," he said with a coy smile.

"Have you ever heard of anything like that?" I asked.

"If you hate him so much, I could hit him," he replied.

"What?" I asked.

"I could hit him for you," he said again.

Ron then asked if he knew anything about the kickbacks the sheriff was receiving from the food distribution company that provided food for jail inmates.

Again, he shook his head.

After more questions and more evasive answers, Ron and I decided to end the interview.

While we were riding back to Birmingham, I asked Ron what he thought Barker meant by saying "I could hit him if you like."

"Who knows?" Ron replied.

"Do you think he was asking if we wanted him to kill the sheriff?" I asked.

"I'm not sure," Ron replied. "All I know is he's a dangerous man."

The following morning, Bloomfield said it was time to talk to the sheriff about the allegations. That afternoon, I called the sheriff's office, spoke with the chief deputy, and scheduled a meeting with the sheriff at Hollister's Café in Smith's Station.

"If anything looks amiss, call me immediately," Bloomfield warned. "This man is capable of anything."

Thanks, PG!

The following afternoon, Ron and I met Sheriff Walton at the appointed time and place. He listened sullenly as we explained the allegations against him, then he reached into his inside coat pocket and pulled out a warrant, which charged both Ron and me with conspiracy to murder him.

Two Sheffield County deputies appeared, frisked and handcuffed us, and took us to jail. At the jail, we learned quickly that four others had been arrested. They were Judge Tyler, our source, "Cowboy" Cochran, Bill Jenkins, the sheriff's opponent in the upcoming election, and his campaign manager. In short, the sheriff had arrested everyone present at the meeting with Jimmy Barker. We were all charged with conspiracy to commit murder against Sheriff Walton.

Judge Tyler, whom Bloomfield had described as the "only honest man in Sheffield County," was the first to be released. Once he was out, he signed the bond for Ron and me.

Back in Birmingham, we were hailed as heroes. Bloomfield called us into his office and explained he was having the attorney general conduct a thorough investigation of the sheriff's charges and had three reporters assigned to a big Sunday spread. He also told us we were scheduled to be at the Alabama Bureau of Investigation office in Montgomery the following afternoon for lie detector tests.

When we arrived for the test, the examiner, who had tested Jimmy Barker earlier, said with a smile, "I know how this is going to turn out."

We learned later that, once we scheduled the interview with Jimmy Barker, he had gone straight to the sheriff and told him about the meeting. Upon learning that Barker was meeting with us, Sheriff Walton instructed him to drop hints to us about assassinating him. Barker was obligated to do the sheriff's bidding because the sheriff had been protecting him from an impending murder charge in Marion County.

The *Age-Herald*'s next Sunday edition blared the headline: "Not a shred of evidence to Sheriff Walton's Charges." The story explained that the state attorney general had conducted a thorough investigation of the sheriff's charges and they had been totally trumped up. The election was five days away.

Two nights before the election, the sheriff held a big rally in Smith's Station. He told the crowd that the *Age-Herald* "had it in for him." He said his long-time political enemy Judge Tyler and "those long-hair reporters" had conspired with the *Age-Herald* to "kill me politically."

The crowd roared its approval. He had become a hero for standing up to the big-city newspaper in Birmingham. The following night at another rally in nearby Sardis, he told a crowd of supporters the same story.

"Walton! Walton! Walton!" the crowd shouted in unison.

The following Tuesday, at the polls, the sheriff won a resounding victory. Our investigation and arrest had had little or no effect on voters. They saw us as outside troublemakers "playing politics" with their sheriff. At that point, I realized that "truth" is relative to who was hearing it.

*****

I was beyond disappointed. I had put my life and reputation on the line for people who had no interest in ridding themselves of their resident evil. In my heart, I had always felt, if a crusading newspaper exposed corruption, voters would join the fight to rid themselves of it. I was devastated that the cancer in Sheffield County was just as alive and well after the investigation as it was before. Ron and I had upheld "the highest tradition of American journalism," but the voting populace had decided Ron and I were nothing more than "long-haired, hippie troublemakers." All those years, I had believed in the power of daily newspapers to expose

Thanks, PG!

corruption. Now those dreams had been dashed. Most importantly, I was devastated that we had failed to get justice for little Elena Torres. The episode had been a huge learning lesson for me.

Some two months later, I was covering a city council meeting in Midfield. Before the meeting started, Chuck Milligan, a reporter with the *Birmingham Herald*, the city's morning newspaper, made a beeline for me.

"I won't be seeing you again," he said, offering his hand. "I'm leaving the *Herald*."

"Where are you going?" I asked.

"I'm going to work for the *National Insider*."

It didn't ring a bell.

"How much will you be making?"

"Starting salary is $22,000," he said. "If they like me, I go to $27,000 after the first six months."

"You're kidding!" I said with total disbelief. Both of us were making around $10,000 a year.

"It's true!" he said.

"If they need someone else, let me know," I replied.

"I will," he said, shaking my hand.

I dismissed the matter.

A month later, the *Age-Herald* printed a small, front-page wire story about an American Navy Admiral who had an affair with a Russian Woman during World War II. When the war was over, she was pregnant and, before he returned stateside, they agreed to continue their relationship and to name the child Victor if it was a boy and Victoria if a girl. It was a wonderful story that explained how the admiral had recently visited Russia to meet his daughter Victoria for the first time. The *National Insider* had published the story. That rang a bell.

"That's where Milligan works now," replied the Metro Editor when I asked. "That place is something else. They'll go anywhere in the world to get a story."

That night, I did some research. The *National Insider* was a tabloid-sized scandal sheet I had seen in drugstores as a child. In those days, the publication featured lurid stories about celebrity gossip, sex crimes, sensational murders, UFOs, alien abductions, and photos of horrific auto accidents. After Sheffield County, I laughed with delight at the thought of working for such a publication.

Two weeks later, I was sitting in the newsroom at the *Age-Herald* when the phone rang.

"May I speak with Billy Don Johnson?" a heavily accented British voice said on the other end of the line.

"Speaking!" I replied.

The caller was Simon Reagan, an editor at the *National Insider*. After explaining he had spoken with Chuck, he said he was impressed with my reputation and asked if I'd be interested in coming to Rosebud, Florida for a two-week tryout.

I answered in the affirmative.

Chapter 4

Tryouts I

Talk about a country boy going to town. That was what my two-week tryout at the *National Insider* was like. Two days before my tryout was to begin, Simon's secretary called to discuss my itinerary. I'd be staying at the Ambassador Hotel in South Palm Beach, flying first-class from Birmingham to Palm Beach International, and a full-sized sedan would be waiting upon arrival. All I had to do, she said, was pack my bags, go to the airport, and get on the flight. All expenses were being paid by the *Insider*.

As instructed, I was on the plane at the appointed time. Not only had I never been on a big commercial airliner before, but I had never flown first class. My previous flying experience was on small two- and four-seat planes going to college football games or viewing clear cuts with the Alabama Forestry Commission. Once the plane landed, I got the rental car and went directly to the hotel. Simon had promised to meet me in the hotel bar at five p.m.

Simon Reagan was a blondish boy of a man in his late thirties. He spoke with a strong English accent and had a small mustache, which he loved to tweak thoughtfully as he swilled down gin and tonics. As soon as I met him, I detected he had an easy felicity for words. I liked that. I immediately wanted to know him better. A native of Stratford in East London, Simon spoke quietly of his lonely childhood in the London suburbs, where he spent long hours trying to entertain himself while his mother was away at work. Deserted by his father at an early age, Simon said his mother Cornelia was one of Dylan Thomas' mistresses, and he recalled that the famous poet had once slapped him during a drunken rage.

All the time he spoke of his childhood, he would tweak his mustache and stare off into space like a little boy who was daydreaming. His reveries were something magical to me. As he droned on and on with his east London accent, I found myself being transported back in time to England's Lake District during the days of Byron, Keats, and Shelly. Somehow, in my mind's eye, I envisioned Keats sitting under a mulberry tree writing "Ode to a Nightingale" or Gerard Manley Hopkins standing at a point overlooking the North Sea and spying the lone wind hover that inspired his famous poem.

After wandering across Europe as a teenager, Simon returned to London in the late sixties and got a job as a copy clerk on Fleet Street. After eleven years, he had risen to a mid-level reporter's position with one of the major Fleet Street dailies when he was called by Alan McDonald, the *Insider*'s executive editor, who invited him to come to Rosebud for a tryout. The reason he was brought from London to the *Insider* was that he had successfully planted a bug in the headboard of the bed that a famous British soccer star and his new bride had slept in while visiting Sydney, Australia. An editor at the *Insider* for almost two years, Simon was four months, from January to April, older than I.

Finally, the conversation turned to the *Insider*.

"Everything is for PG," he began. "The entire publication is created by and for Mr. Padrone Gallione, otherwise known as PG. It's solely for his entertainment, amusement, and enrichment. He's the maestro and we're the marionettes."

Simon explained the original publication known as the *National Insider* had been owned by Mr. Gallione's father in

Thanks, PG!

New York. Padrone Gallione Sr. had originally purchased the newspaper with $100,000 he'd borrowed from long-time mobster Anthony "Fat Tony" Gravano with the stipulation he would publish nothing about mobsters. After the publication gained moderate success in New York and his father passed, PG moved the publication to south Florida in the early seventies. In keeping with his great admiration of William Randolph Hearst, he purchased the land and founded and incorporated the city of Rosebud, Florida to serve as the publication's world headquarters. Simon said PG's dream was to leave his mark on American journalism in the same tradition as Hearst.

"How is he going to do that with a scandal sheet?" I asked.

He didn't answer at first.

"Mr. Gallione feels that tabloid subjects should be as much of part of America's information diet as politics, sports, and financial information."

I waited for his words to register.

"There's much more to the *Insider* than meets the eye," he continued. "The *Insider* is more or less of a hobby for PG. Although he makes millions with the *Insider*, PG is also a true intellectual who's interested in understanding the great philosophical problems of the ages. You realize that PG is an engineer, a lawyer, and a doctor?"

"He has degrees in all three?" I asked.

Simon nodded. "Engineering degree is from MIT," he said. "Law and medical degrees from Harvard."

"He must be intelligent," I said.

"He's eccentric," Simon said flatly. "That's for sure, but he's also a genius. The rewards of knowing the genius far outweigh the frustrations of dealing with the eccentricities."

I had heard what he said, but somehow, I still doubted the words. I had no evidence to the contrary. I simply doubted the things he was telling me. It was too unbelievable.

"Billy Don," he said finally, "there is no quick, easy definition for life at the *Insider*. Most important, you can't understand the nature of the publication just by looking at its cover. You'll just have to come and live in PG's world and see if you like it. And rest assured," he added emphatically, "it's not for everybody."

I laughed.

"You may laugh," Simon continued seriously, "but you'll not be bored. I promise you that. The *Insider* is a journalistic adventure like no other. And nobody, I mean nobody, pays more money."

He studied me for a moment.

Suddenly, someone called Simon's name and he turned. It was the hotel desk clerk telling him his wife had arrived to take him home.

"Okay, mate!" he said, offering his hand. "I must depart this sad vale of tears."

I laughed at his casual theatrical behavior.

"You've got two weeks to prove yourself to me and PG," he said. "See you tomorrow at the office."

That night, as I crawled under the covers of the king-sized bed at the luxurious Ambassador Hotel, I wondered what madness I was about to embark upon. I didn't have a clue as to where I was headed, but I loved what I had seen so far. Before I went to sleep, it suddenly dawned on me that tomorrow morning I'd be working for a newspaper that was founded with mafia money! *Now that's rich,* I thought. It all seemed so unreal. I felt like I had wandered into a dream.

*****

The next morning, I was up early, showered, shaved, had breakfast at the hotel restaurant, and headed to the *Insider* office for the first time. En route, I stopped in the Rosebud

Thanks, PG!

town square. There, in the center of the square, stood a marble statue of PG peering eastward toward the ocean and looking wise and visionary. At the base of the statue was a plaque, which read: *"Rosebud, Florida, founded August 2, 1970 by Padrone Gallione."* At the bottom, in big letters, was inscribed: *"He brought pleasure to millions."*

When I arrived at the office, Simon met me at the door and introduced me to Laura, the tall, thin, hatchet-faced woman who coordinated the needs of the reporters with the business office. She assigned me a cubicle in the "bullpen," the area designated for reporters, then delivered pens, notebooks, a tape recorder, and a typewriter, which I signed for. My cubicle was a four-by-four work area that faced the outside. Once seated and looking out the massive plate glass windows, I could see the tall, verdant royal palms surrounding the building, the Florida Central Railroad tracks just beyond the palms, and Dixie Highway, the famous route that connected New York and Miami. Intermixed with the royal palms were an equal number of Florida loblolly pines and squirrels, hundreds upon hundreds, nested and lived among their spreading branches.

Once I settled in, I started to introduce myself to the other reporters. In the cubicle to my left sat a tall, dark-haired American from Kentucky named John Harris. Affable, talkative, and forever happy, John said he had just returned from an around-the-world assignment in search of paradise. Over a two-month period, he said he had visited twenty-eight of the world's most exotic islands, including the Shetlands, the Hebrides, the Greek and Spanish Islands, and most of the South Sea islands, including Bora Bora, in search of mankind's oldest fantasy. I asked if the story was published.

"Oh, no," he replied. "It was a personal story for PG."

"A what?"

"A personal story for the boss," he continued. "PG wanted to know if paradise really existed, so he assigned me to travel the world to try and find it."

I shook my head in disbelief.

In the cubicle behind me sat a thin, older man named Jim Temmey, who had a shaved head, a quick wit, and was forever chomping on an unlit cigar. He said he'd worked for *National Geographic* for eight years before joining the *Insider* and had just returned from Nepal, where he'd spent a month with Sherpa guides searching for the Himalayan Sasquatch.

Again, I was in disbelief that reporters were being assigned stories like that.

Around eleven a.m., Simon called me into his office and said we needed to get started with my "retraining." Every *Insider* story begins with a headline, he began. With daily newspapers, the story is written first, then edited, and the headline is written last.

"At the *Insider*," he said, "the headline is written first and the central focus of the story and everything contained within the story must logically support the headline."

Simon peered at me for a long moment as if he were waiting for his statement to register.

"Your first assignment is a government waste story," he said finally, handing me a file folder.

I opened the folder.

Bold type screamed the headline: "Senator blasts US Government Agency for wasting $285,000 to study rare Texas cockroach." Included in the folder was a magazine clip providing details of how the National Institute of Health had granted $285,000 to a university in the Midwest to study the habitat, breeding habits, migration patterns, and food sources of the rare blue-winged cockroach.

Thanks, PG!

"It's a straightforward story," Simon said. "Interview the senator's publicist. Get strong quotes on his outrage and fill in details as needed. Give me about eight to ten paragraphs."

I took the file.

"What's a personal story for PG?" I asked.

"Oh, PG gets a wild hair from time to time," he replied. "He sends reporters to the ends of the earth to answer some crazy question that popped into his head. Some of the guys have gotten great trips out of those."

I got up to leave.

"One more thing," he said. "We're having lunch at the Ambassador today. I want you to meet my other tryouts."

I nodded and closed the door.

Back at my cubicle, I read the file and put in calls to the senator's publicist in Washington. I jotted down exact questions to ask and wrote out a bare-bones intro for the story.

At lunch that day, I met Simon's other two tryouts. Wayne Winkenhoffer, a medium-built, dark-haired man in his late twenties who recently lost his job as a police reporter with a small Kansas daily, said his lifelong dream was to work for the *Insider*.

"I'm going to make my tryouts if it kills me," he said, running his hand jauntily through his wavy, unkempt hair.

His family owned a chain of funeral homes in Kansas, and he explained that, if he didn't make his tryouts, he was destined to spend the rest of his life in funeral homes. He said he was poring over magazines and newspapers every night and turning in around twenty-five story leads a day. His eyes looked like a Georgia roadmap and, from the smell, he hadn't had a recent bath. As he talked, I could see a slight nervous twitch in his chin. Wayne was stressed to the max.

Simon's other tryout was Rona Lee Steinman, an early-forties divorcee from Simi Valley, California. The mother of two teenage girls, she'd been the long-time society editor of a small community newspaper in the San Fernando Valley. Like Wayne, she spent night after night scouring various publications for story ideas. Rona Lee, who was also staying at the Ambassador, said she'd never seen so many stressed-out people in her entire life. She referred to her *Insider* tryout as "paranoia in the palms." We agreed to have dinner that night at the hotel restaurant.

After lunch, I returned to the office, did the interview with the senator's publicist, and started writing the story. As I sat typing, I watched through the window as the endless parade of chattering squirrels frolicked to and fro along the narrow window ledge. There were so many squirrels and the ledge was so narrow that often one would get bumped off to the sidewalk below. Like little humans, they would stand on their hind legs, put their little paws on the plate glass, and flash their solid-white bellies as if they were watching me. I imagined they were minions of PG telling me to write a good story with meaty quotes and blaring headlines to help get circulation up for the *Insider*. There was no end to the surrealism of the place.

Late that afternoon, I proudly presented the government waste story to Simon. He said we'd go through it the following morning.

That night, I had dinner with Rona Lee. We ate, had drinks, and walked on the beach afterward. She had some dynamite weed and God knows I needed it. Weed can take a person away from themselves with virtually no side effects or collateral damage. All human beings who are achievers tend to become stressed as a result of their pursuits. Everybody needs some form of physical release from this stress. Weed not only takes one away from oneself, but it presents a person to him or herself in the most objective light imaginable. It's a special learning tool that allows one to gather self-knowledge. Alcohol never allowed me that luxury.

Thanks, PG!

During the walk on the beach, she and I engaged in some lightweight cuddling, which we later consummated back in her hotel room. Post-coitus, she predicted that Wayne was going to implode from all the stress of the tryout.

"He's a nut case," she said. "He's capable of doing anything at any time."

I looked at her.

"I'm serious," she continued. "He's a time bomb waiting to explode."

When I crawled into bed that night, I knew I wanted this job more than anything I had ever wanted. Not only did I want it with all of my heart and soul, but I was prepared to do whatever was necessary to get it.

Next morning at the office, Simon and I went through the government waste story.

"You're going to have to forget most, not all, of what you've learned working for American newspapers," he said. "The essential story you've given me is for an American newspaper, not the *Insider*."

Simon said, most important, I had to learn "Insiderese," the colorful, snappy language unique to the *Insider*.

"It's a language all its own," he said.

He handed me two copies of the government waste story; the one I had written and the one he had rewritten in "Insiderese."

"We're going to compare your version with the 'Insiderese' version," he said. "Read the first paragraph of your copy."

I read it aloud. "A Wisconsin senator has expressed concern that the National Institute of Health wasted $285,000 in a grant to study a rare cockroach."

"Now read my version," he said.

"A world-famous U.S. senator is mad as hell because the National Institute of Health has blown away a whopping

$285,000 to study the love life of some cockamamie cockroach, the *Insider* has learned."

"The study was also about migration habits and food sources," I protested, "not just the mating habits."

"For the *Insider*, you must select and emphasize the sexy, the titillating, and the exciting. That's what *Insider* readers want. Bring emotion and a colorful flair to your copy. *Insider* readers could care less about their migration habits and food sources. That's the kind of thinking that makes you a good reporter at the *Insider*. That's the way PG thinks and that's how you should think."

He proceeded to go through the rest of my story, explaining how each element had been changed to meet *Insider* standards. Once finished, I knew he was right. It had been a good lesson.

That night, I joined Simon and his English colleagues for drinks in the Ambassador bar. His closest friend was Clive Fuller, a stocky, balding Englishman in his early forties, who was also an editor and had once been knocked down by the Queen's horses while trying to get a photo of Her Highness in her royal carriage. Simon's second friend was Bob Stevens, a tall, forever happy former Fleet Streeter who worked as an airbrush artist in the photo department. While nursing their drinks, the three loved to regale themselves with memories of living in England, stories about their families, and endless tales about PG and his eccentricities. After listening quietly for almost an hour, I asked a question.

"When do I get to meet PG?"

Bob laughed out loud at my question.

"Believe me," he said mysteriously, "it's nothing to look forward to."

This brought more laughs from Simon and Clive.

"You'll meet PG when you finish your tryout," Simon said. "Reporters seldom, if ever, see him. Most of the time, he stays

Thanks, PG!

tucked away in his private office, the 'Inner Sanctum.' He meets with the editors every day in his office, but seldom comes out on the floor."

The following morning, Simon called me into this office first thing.

"Do you know anything about medicine?" he asked.

"I studied pharmacy for four years and worked five years in a hospital," I said off-handedly.

"Holy Christ," Simon said excitedly. "You never told me that."

"You never asked," I replied.

"You understand molecular structure, symptoms, side effects, and such?"

I nodded.

"Go to the library, go through the major medical magazines, and find some leads about promising new drugs. Look particularly close at the *New England Journal of Medicine* and the AMA monthlies. Quickest way to search is to scan the titles under the table of contents. I'd love to have two, maybe three, good medical leads," he said.

That afternoon, I went to the Palm Beach County library and launched into the medical magazines and, after two hours, found two articles about promising new drugs. One was a story about a new diabetes drug that was absorbed into the bloodstream much faster than existing medications. Another was a promising new drug derived from the nightshade plant which, in clinical trials, was shown to slow metastasis in cancer patients. Late that afternoon, I typed up the leads and presented them to Simon.

"PG will love the one about the diabetes drug," he predicted.

*****

That night, as I gazed across the hotel courtyard toward the ocean, I could feel the intense pressure of the tryout taking its toll. As long as I was engaged in the daily routine of the job, I somehow didn't notice the extent of the stress. At night, however, when I was away from the office, the stress of directing, then redirecting my energies each and every moment toward a single goal was grinding on me.

Suddenly, I saw Rona Lee pulling into the parking area below. I raced down the steps to meet her.

"Any herb?"

"Only the best!" she replied.

I could have kissed her.

The next morning, when I arrived at the office, Simon handed me the approved lead sheet on the new diabetes drug.

"Remember, on a medical story, you've got to have five things for PG," he said. "The generic name for the new drug, the molecular structure, its mechanism of action, indications, and side effects. All of this has to come either from a drug researcher or some documentation."

That afternoon, I interviewed one of the lead researchers on the project, who provided a full explanation as to indications, mechanism of action, and side effects. After some delay contacting the FDA for comment, I finally finished writing and filed the story late Thursday.

That night, at the hotel bar, Simon said, "You do know a lot about medicine."

"Thanks," I said.

"I didn't tell you this earlier," he said, "but most *Insider* reporters are afraid to do medical stories."

"Why?" I asked.

"You must remember that PG is a physician," he replied. "When you file a medical story, you have to have all of your facts and figures nailed down with all of the fully-qualified details. If you don't have those details, you're in deep crapola."

Thanks, PG!

"What happens?"

"Several times, reporters have filed a medical story that didn't have complete documentation and PG had questions. When they were unable to answer PG's questions, they were fired."

"You think I'll get called in to answer questions?"

He shook his head and laughed out loud.

"You had everything PG required," he said. "I made sure of that before I gave him the story. PG approved the story for publication before he left the office today."

I breathed a sigh of relief. I had heard from people wiser than me that anything learned in life will be used at some point. Many times, I had wondered how my pharmacy training would be useful in my daily life. Incredibly, I had found it!

"Next week is the last week of your tryout," Simon said before I left the office on Friday. "Try to have me some good medical leads for Monday morning."

Chapter 5

Tryouts II

That weekend, I spent all day Saturday and Sunday at the local library searching for leads. I was at the library when it opened at nine on Saturday and finished when it closed at five p.m. Sunday afternoon. By Sunday night, I had thirty-eight story leads.

The following morning, I handed in the new leads. Simon giggled with delight, then thumbed through a stack of files, carefully selected one, and handed it to me. It was a rags-to-riches tale about a man who had gone from being dirt-poor to owning one of the largest apple orchards in the world. Simon said he would like to have it on Tuesday. That afternoon, after all of the other reporters had gone home, I worked until almost six p.m. in the office to finish it.

As I typed away, a serious-looking man, maybe five foot eight, medium-built, in his early fifties, came wandering back to "the bullpen." Dressed in a plain, blue-checkered shirt and light brown pants, he peered along the ceiling line where the air-conditioning vents were located. From the dark stains on his fingers, I could see he was a heavy smoker, and he had a pocket protector with an assortment of pens and pencils inside.

Finally, he turned to look at me. As my eyes met his, I was suddenly jolted by his gaze. I felt a cold shudder up and down my spine and quickly averted my eyes. For several minutes, I

Thanks, PG!

pretended to be concentrating on the story and feared to look back at the man.

Moments later, he turned and walked to the other end of the building. I was glad he was gone. I was still agitated by his piercing stare. As I peered after him, I wondered who he was. Never in my entire life had anyone looked at me like that. It was as if he was peering into my very soul. Finally, I concluded he was the supervisor of the cleaning crew and was checking the quality of their work.

The following morning, Simon was happy with the rags-to-riches story and said he sent it straight to "the boss." After I returned to my desk, I was chatting with another reporter when, suddenly, the office quiet was pierced with a bloodcurdling scream.

Instantly, everyone's attention turned to the scream. It was Wayne. As Rona Lee had predicted, the sleepless nights, the stress of the tryouts, and the fear of working in a funeral home for the rest of his life had finally taken its toll.

"My legs! My legs!" he screamed. "I can't move my legs."

Simon came over. After hearing the screaming, executive editor Alan McDonald came out of his office. The other reporters gathered around and peered down at Wayne writhing in agony on the newsroom floor. Simon and McDonald helped him to his feet, but when they released him, he fell to the floor again, screaming in agony. Finally, Simon called the county emergency medical services and Wayne was removed from the office in a wheelchair. That was the last we heard of him.

*****

That night, after Wayne's implosion, the topic of discussion at the Ambassador bar was stories about tryouts. Bob said the *Insider* once had an editor, a pudgy little Englishwoman named Sally Godwin, who could "really knock 'em back." One night, she was out drinking with another editor and a tryout named Eric Johansen. They had left one bar and were cruising down the coast highway in the editor's Mercedes in search of another bar. As they rode, they were laughing, talking and regaling one another when suddenly, the driver "overcorrected" and the Mercedes ran off the highway into the Intracoastal Waterway. The Mercedes, which had landed in some thirty feet of water, started to sink rapidly.

"Get me out of here! Get me out of here!" Sally screamed. "I can't swim!"

The tryout, Eric, who had grown up in Los Angeles and spent his teenage years as a surfer at Malibu, climbed out of the Mercedes, pulled the frantic Sally out of the car, and swam to shore with her. The Mercedes was fully submerged by the time the tryout managed to get her to shore.

Once they were onshore, Eric could see she had stopped breathing. Eric, by virtue of his surfing experience, gave her mouth-to-mouth resuscitation and she started breathing again. Essentially, Eric had saved her life. Two weeks later, when his tryout ended, she didn't approve him and he went back to free-lancing in Los Angeles.

"My favorite tryout story was about Paul Rothstein and Sylvia Goldman," Simon said.

Every spring, PG sent his reps to the big-name universities and colleges in the northeast to recruit "Ivy-league Wonders" as tryouts. PG's minions would canvass MIT, Harvard, Cornell, Vassar, Brown, and other prestigious colleges for candidates. One such tryout was a woman named Sylvia Goldman, a recent Vassar graduate.

Upon her arrival in Rosebud, Simon said she was assigned to Paul Rothstein, a long-time editor and a fat pig of a man. Paul was notorious for brokering jobs for sex with female tryouts and, in fact, the company had been sued twice for such antics. At the end of Sylvia's tryout, Paul told her he would

Thanks, PG!

approve her as a reporter if she would have sex with him on the beach. She agreed. After the deal was struck, she told another reporter about their agreement and, of course, the news spread like wildfire around the office that the great event was to occur the following Friday night on the beach near the Outrigger.

The Outrigger was a beachside hotel that PG occasionally used for tryouts. It was built like a ship with three separate levels. The top level was the crow's nest, a popular place where bar patrons could peer across the Atlantic for almost a mile in either direction. On the night of the big event, half of the office was at the crow's nest to watch fat Paul pounding this little stick of a woman in the surf.

"It was something to behold," Simon said.

*****

On Wednesday morning, I was back at the library, poring over magazines and newspapers. I came up with a lead about the childhood of Einstein, dinner table blunders of the rich and famous, and two leads for category stories. Late that afternoon, I returned to the office and filed the leads.

"Tomorrow is the big day," Simon said. "You're meeting PG tomorrow."

Somehow, when he said the words, I was filled with fear that I would say something wrong in the presence of the great man and fail my tryout. I certainly didn't want to end up like Wayne Winkenhoffer and return to Birmingham to cover city council meetings for the rest of my life.

That night, I ran into Rona Lee again in the hotel restaurant. As I approached her, I could see she'd been crying.

"What's wrong?" I asked, taking a seat at her table.

"I didn't make my tryout," she said sadly. "I'm going back to LA tomorrow."

"I'm sorry to hear that," I said.

After a dinner of shrimp scampi and beer, we walked on the beach for almost an hour. I listened as she cried softly, pouring out her heart. Although she'd had seven story ideas approved, she hadn't had a single story published.

"The whole place is so crazy," she said again and again. "There's no stability. I can never seem to get my feet on the ground."

She said she would return to her society editor's job and write about weddings and births and civic club meetings. The hours were long, the job paid little, and the managing editor was a tyrant, she said, but it would be a relief to see her daughters again and she explained that the older one was planning on being married in the fall.

Finally, she was quiet.

"At least you did better than Wayne Winkenhoffer," I observed.

She smiled through her tears.

"You always find some way to make everything better," she replied.

Finally, as we started up the steps from the beach back to the hotel, she asked me to come to her room and help heal the sorrows of not making her tryout. I told her I thought that could be arranged.

*****

When I arrived at the office the following morning, I was filled with trepidation at meeting PG. After all the stories I had heard and seeing the power he wielded over the lives of so many people, I was filled with fear of the unknown.

At around 9:30, Simon called me into his office.

Thanks, PG!

"We're due to talk to PG in fifteen minutes," he said. "Now, you have to be careful. One misstep and you can blow the entire tryout."

"Even if you're a really good reporter?"

"Yes," he said with dead seriousness. "Don't expect anything logical out of PG. In fact, that's the last thing you should expect."

Simon could see that I was filled with dread.

"Look!" he said sympathetically. "Take a deep breath and calm down. I'm going to tell you exactly what to do in the interview."

"Go ahead," I replied.

"The boss is a generous man," Simon said, "but he doesn't like to be disagreed with. So, point number one, don't do anything to disagree with him."

I nodded.

"No complaints about your accommodations, your hotel, rental car, meals, anything like that."

I nodded.

"Also, don't say anything negative about Italians or New Yorkers."

I nodded.

"Don't say anything about blondes," he said. "His wife is a blonde, so no blonde jokes."

I nodded.

"Respond only to his questions," Simon said. "No innocent observations, side comments, cute quotations, or anything like that. Be all business."

I nodded.

"Just remember, I'll be sitting right beside you," he said. "If I bump you with my knee, shut up immediately."

"Got it!" I said.

"Let's go to the 'Inner Sanctum.'"

He stopped.

"One more thing," Simon said. "If he shows you the photo he had made with P.T Barnum, try to look interested."

I nodded for the last time.

"Let's go!"

Moments later, Simon escorted me down a hallway past a bank of exquisitely appointed executive offices. At the end of the hallway, I could see a set of double doors. The sign read *Padrone Gallione.*

Behind the doors, we were greeted by a secretary, a small, dark-haired Italian woman. Simon announced we were there to see Mr. Gallione. She hit the button on an intercom and announced our intentions.

"Send them in!" we heard a voice say.

PG's office was truly something to behold. Decorated in various hues of blue and green, the focal point was a massive, circular mahogany desk some twenty feet across. Stack after stack of story files were scattered across the room and, beyond the desk, I could see the finely manicured *Insider* grounds, the railroad tracks, and Dixie Highway.

Immediately behind the desk was a huge bronze statue of William Randolph Hearst pointing into the distance and, behind it, on the wall, in three-foot-high letters, was emblazoned the words *"Most people live vicariously!"* A model train track, complete with passenger stations, loading docks, and countryside scenery, ran across the desk, up the wall, and around the entire office. Directly above the desk was a giant glass dome, which served as a skylight.

The moment Simon and I entered, we could see a man in one corner with his back turned to us. He was tinkering with the model train tracks that circumvented the office. Finally, when he turned, I was shocked. This was the same man I had seen in "the bullpen" earlier in the week. He was the guy I thought was in charge of the cleaning crew. I couldn't believe it! This was PG, the godfather? The grand wizard? This is the

Thanks, PG!

man so universally feared and worshipped? He looked so unwizardly!

"Good morning!" he greeted, taking a seat behind the mahogany desk.

"Mr. Gallione, this is Billy Don Johnson," Simon said.

"Good morning, Billy Don," he said in an almost fatherly tone. "Have a seat!"

Simon and I seated ourselves side by side, facing the desk. Above our heads, a fresh, light Florida rain was pounding down on the glass dome.

Glancing up at the steady rain, PG seemed annoyed. He flipped open a console unit on the desk and pushed a switch. Instantly, the steady raindrops splaying against the glass dome above us disappeared and bright Florida sunlight washed through the office. I was amazed. I looked at Simon. He shifted his eyes nervously as a warning. I tried to remain calm.

Simon handed him my file.

"Now let's see, Billy Don," PG said, putting on his glasses.

We remained quiet while he studied my file.

"You've done well," he said finally. "You've had three stories published and seven leads approved, one of which will become a new story category."

He flashed a faint smile.

I felt uneasy.

"Billy Don, do you believe in UFOs?"

"Yes, sir!" I replied. "I believe there's the possibility of life on other planets."

He pursed his lips with satisfaction.

"Billy Don, there are a few things you have to understand about the *Insider*," he said. "Our publication appears to be news, but it's not news. It's entertainment. Does that make sense?"

"Yes, sir!"

"We provide lives to people who don't have a life," he continued. "We bring excitement, entertainment, and useful information to people whose lives would be dull and boring without us. Do you understand what I'm saying?"

"Yes, sir!" I replied.

He studied me again for a long moment. I was still afraid to look into his eyes. He turned to an object on his desk.

"Billy Don," he started, "I want to show you a photo I had made with the great showman P.T. Barnum."

He picked up the photo from the desk and displayed it for me. The photo was taken on Coney Island, and it showed an older man in a business suit shaking hands with a young, dark-haired child.

Simon bumped my knee and I stepped forward.

"It's a nice photo," I said, trying to appear interested.

Satisfied I had done my duty, I took a seat again.

"I was nine years old," PG said, peering wistfully at the photo. "I love that photo."

Finally, he returned the photo to his desk and studied me for a long moment.

"You know, many years ago, I worked in the South when I was with the CIA," he continued. "I spent three years at Oakridge, Tennessee and I can recognize a Tennessee accent a mile away. What part of Tennessee are you from?"

"Actually, Mr. Gallione—" I began.

Suddenly, Simon bumped my knee again. It was the signal to shut up.

"Billy Don is from Nashville," Simon said quickly. "He grew up just outside of Nashville, home of the Grand Ole Opry."

PG pursed his lips and nodded with pure satisfaction.

"Isn't there a major river that runs near Nashville?" he asked off-handedly. "Isn't that the Cumberland?"

Simon nudged my knee.

Thanks, PG!

"Yes, sir!" I replied nervously. "I believe that's correct."

PG pursed his lips again and nodded his satisfaction. For a long, pregnant moment, he glared at me. Suddenly, I felt myself starting to physically tremble. I tried to calm myself by holding my breath. Finally, he spoke.

"Billy Don, I think you'll be an asset to us," he said.

I exhaled. "Thank you, Mr. Gallione," I replied nervously.

"Welcome aboard," he said with finality.

Simon and I shook hands with him again and left the office.

The meeting had been so fast and so final that, as Simon and I walked back down the hallway to the newsroom, I was walking in a daze. I had actually met the great wizard and survived. I was now an official reporter at the *National Insider*. The realization didn't sink in until I left the office for lunch. Once outside, I gave a huge fist pump to the sunny Florida skies and shouted, "Yesssssssssss!"

My first two weeks at the *Insider* had been more unbelievable and surrealistic than anything I could ever have imagined. The one and only thing I had come to expect from the place was the unexpected. The madness I had yearned for had been delivered. More than anything, the wild man hiding inside me all those years was about to be set free. I couldn't wait!

John Isaac Jones

Chapter 6

The City of PG

So "The Tall Guy from Tennessee" was born. Like everything else at the *Insider*, I was just a figment of the publisher's imagination, just another player in the surreal fantasy of a madman, another munchkin in this make-believe world known as the *National Insider*. But, oh, what a wonderfully sweet madness it was; a madness so replete with surprise and innocence and greed and adventure and downright stupidity that I knew I could never extricate myself.

When I arrived at the office the following morning, Simon sent me directly to the business office to get my "credentials and credit cards." The business office was located on the opposite end of the building from the editorial department and, as I strolled down the canopied walkway past the royal palms, the dwarf loblolly pines, and the pink, yellow, and white camellias, I felt like a king marching down a red carpet to his throne.

Walking into the *Insider* business office was like stepping onto the set of a mafia movie. As I walked past the executive offices, I noticed that the names on the nameplates all ended in a vowel. There were names like Cuomo, Napolitano, Graziano, Corleone, and Costello.

The business manager, a tall Italian man wearing thick glasses and chomping on an unlit cigar, was cordial. He shook my hand and welcomed me into his office. After I sat down,

Thanks, PG!

he produced a *National Insider* ID badge, a box of business cards, a thousand-dollar cash advance, and credit cards. There was a top-flight blue and white credit card, universal airline card, and hotel and rental car cards. As I started back to the newsroom, I thought, *Oh great God, I've died and gone to heaven.*

I remember once at the *Age-Herald*, I was on a stakeout trying to get a photo of a politician meeting his bagman at a shopping center. I was standing on the side of a hill in the rain and, when the bagman parked his car, I couldn't see the exchange, so I raced down the hill a ways for a better perspective. En route, I sank up to my ankles in mud and ruined my socks, so I turned in an expense report for the loss. Three weeks later, I was called into the managing editor's office and was told, "Mr. Johnson, we don't buy socks for our reporters."

These people had just handed me the equivalent of ten thousand dollars without blinking an eye.

That night, I had drinks with Simon, Clive, and Bob at the Ambassador lounge.

"How did he change the weather from rain to sunshine?" I asked Simon.

"I don't have a clue," he replied. "Once, I was in his office, and he was trying to light a cigarette, and the lighter wouldn't work. He threw the lighter into the trash, then flipped his thumb against his forefinger and lit the cigarette."

"Bull crap!" I said.

He shrugged again.

"Look, mate," he said, "if you don't believe that, then never ask me how he changed rain to sunshine. He just did it. Okay?"

I shook my head in disbelief.

*****

The die had been cast and I settled into the *Insider*. Over the next year, I learned tabloid reporting from top to bottom. In the newspaper business, editors and publishers had traditionally been two distinct positions. The publisher oversaw the total operation. His job was to keep all of the separate departments—newsroom, advertising, circulation, photography, composing room etc.—coordinated and running smoothly. The editor, on the other hand, was responsible for overseeing the news operation. He hired and fired reporters, directed editorial policy, insured that all necessary newsroom resources were available and, generally, did for the newsroom what the publisher did for the entire organization.

In PG's case, he had combined the editor's job and publisher's job into one person. He not only ran the business, but he personally monitored every single iota of content in the publication. Whether it was headlines, photos, layouts, or fillers, PG kept a watchful eye on the entire operation to insure that quality was always at the highest level. He even checked the spelling of the words in the classified ads.

In the company pecking order, PG was at the top. His second in command was Alan McDonald, a tall, squeaky-voiced Scotsman who was probably the most hated executive editor who ever lived.

McDonald's assistant was Colin Wellesley, another Scotsman equally hated by Simon and the other editors. Wellesley was generally referred to as "McDonald's axe-man" since he was the one who handled McDonald's firings. The next level down the ladder was the articles editors, and there could be anywhere from eight to fifteen at any given time. Under the editors were reporters, and last in line were free-lancers.

Over the next year, I learned the *Insider* editorial operation from top to bottom. "The system," the employees' pet name

Thanks, PG!

for PG's story-manufacturing operation, was a four-layered pyramid with PG at the top. New leads or story ideas could be submitted by anyone—reporters, writers, secretaries, editors, freelancers, or the man in the moon—but they had to be approved by PG before any action was taken.

Once PG approved a lead, it went back to the editor, who submitted it, and the story was then assigned to a reporter. Once the reporter filed the story, it went to an evaluator, who determined how many pages the final written story was worth in tabloid terms. Once tabloid value was determined, the story went to the writers for composition. Once written, the story went to PG's desk for final approval and placement in the publication.

Early on, I determined I was lucky to be working for Simon. He was not only one of PG's most ardent devotees, he also had an in-depth understanding of tabloid journalism. Nobody could sum up the essence of the *Insider* quite like Simon. Some nights at the Ambassador bar, after seven or eight gin and tonics, he had absolute flashes of genius.

"Most people on this earth wouldn't have a life if it wasn't for media," Simon would say. "Newspapers, magazines, television, books, movies—all of these different types of media are essential adjuncts to human lives. This means that we, as information providers, must create a world for them. At the *Insider*, we must create a world that is as interesting, entertaining, and as helpful to their daily lives as possible. Every story in the *Insider* fulfills some special need in the reader.

"Fat people love to read about dieting," he said. "It gives them hope. Hungry people like to read about food. Horny people like to read about sex. Curious people like to read about UFOs, the paranormal, and the supernatural. A story about some famous celebrity who was embarrassed or hurt or has personal problems cuts them down to size. These stories bring celebrities down off their pedestals and show the reader that famous people are human like the rest of us.

"Each and every *Insider* edition fulfills a vast array of human needs," Simon would conclude, explaining that PG had the "exact recipe" week after week for fulfilling those needs.

The single commodity for which there was no shortage at the *Insider* was money. In fact, at times, it seemed money was like paper clips. There was plenty for everybody as long as it was used productively to further the publication. Journalists at the *Insider* were well aware that no other publication in the world paid higher salaries or offered better benefits. If that wasn't enough, expenses accounts boggled the imagination.

*****

One afternoon, when I arrived back at the office from lunch, a frantic Simon met me at the door.

"Quick! Quick!" he said urgently. "You've got to be in Oklahoma City tonight!"

"What's going on?" I asked.

"There was an explosion at a firecracker factory near Oklahoma City and PG wants a story for this edition. We lock up tomorrow afternoon."

"I'm not even packed," I said. "I don't have underwear, shaving gear, or clean socks."

"You've got credit cards," he said. "Buy a suitcase, clothes, and everything else you need for the trip. This is for PG, and no expenses are spared."

I drove to the airport, got on a plane, and bought everything I needed once I arrived in Oklahoma City. The only item I took with me was a portable typewriter. The total bill for suitcase, new clothes, underwear, shaving gear, etc. was twelve hundred dollars. When I turned in the expense report, it sailed right through.

Thanks, PG!

Of course, with such an extravagant expense policy, there was plenty of room for abuse. Many reporters would save up their dry cleaning for a trip, then take the clothes on the trip and get them dry-cleaned for free. There were thousands of cases where reporters would forge receipts for meals, cab rides, hotel rooms, and reporter supplies. According to one story, a reporter bought a luxury condo in South Palm Beach with money he had scammed from his expense account.

Also, there was limitless money for sources. Being able to offer money to sources for information opened up a whole new dynamic for a reporter. If a source had information needed for a story and there was no financial incentive, that source had to have some compelling reason to provide the information. He had to either like the reporter personally or have some interest in the results of publishing the information.

Ultimately, there was always the possibility the source might not divulge the information. When paying for information, a reporter had to have a firm, upfront agreement with the source about payment stipulations. Before a source was paid, all his information was vetted against other information the reporter had relative to the story. If the information didn't prove to be true and correct, the informant received no money. Every time I made an agreement to pay for information, I applied the caveat "If the information doesn't check out, you won't get paid."

Of course, paying for information, like expenses, left room for abuse. In one case, one reporter was fired after he had scammed the company for an estimated fifty thousand dollars. Week after week, he was turning in vouchers for sources with fictitious names and having them sent to a mysterious address. Finally, an accounting office audit revealed the checks were being collected by the reporter himself.

If the virtually endless money for salaries, sources, and expenses wasn't enough, staffers could also earn money by submitting leads. An approved lead that resulted in publication earned one hundred dollars for the lead itself and, if it appeared on the front page, there was an additional two-hundred-and-fifty bonus. Rumors were that some editors had leads in "the system" worth up to twenty-five thousand dollars. Some freelancers never wrote stories; they made all of their income from producing leads.

Ultimately, I don't think PG cared about the money, and that was why he was so free with it. He had more money than he could ever spend and he knew that. Although in later years he hired people to monitor expenses, even then, the *Insider* easily had the most liberal expense policies of any publication known to man. The bottom line was, if one devoted oneself to PG and made the *Insider* a more profitable product in the market place, the rewards would be more than adequate.

*****

One dominant facet of the *Insider* was that all employees were forever conscious of the ongoing legend of PG. Each and every day, that legend was being added to and, over time, the scope of the stories reached mythological proportions. It was well known that PG was an engineer, an attorney, and a physician, but he also had a deep interest in world history, anthropology, and genetics.

"There are no borders to this man's intellect," Simon would say. "His mind encompasses the entire spectrum of human knowledge."

Somehow, I thought Simon was pushing the envelope in his descriptions of PG, but the longer I worked at the *Insider*, the truer the descriptions became.

"His memory is truly photographic," Simon would say. "Three months ago, I turned in a lead about a university study that showed cranberry juice was not only a natural antibiotic,

Thanks, PG!

but it was also a natural diuretic. Next morning, he sent the story back with a note that this had been published two years earlier in the May 23, 1973 edition."

Simon said he checked back issues and PG was "exactly right."

His whims were as endless as they were arbitrary.

Clive told the story of PG assigning an editor the task of buying him a yacht.

"How much do you want to spend?" the editor asked.

"Hold it to around a million," PG replied.

The editor was frantic that he might select a vessel that didn't meet PG's approval, so he assigned one of his reporters the task of selecting a yacht. The reporter was Italian, and the editor felt that this qualification would make him best suited to make the purchase. Finally, the reporter spent just over one million dollars to purchase and transport a fifty-two-foot yacht from Portsmouth, Virginia to PG's berth near his beachside home. The vessel sat in the berth for eleven years and PG never boarded it.

PG was forever trying to improve his reporters' performance. Many times, this only added to the surrealism and madness of the place. In the mid-seventies, when TV shows about SWAT teams were popular, PG got the idea to create SWAT teams of reporters that could be instantly mobilized and dispatched to cover news events. Once the teams were in place, they were ready to "attack" their target in record time. I had been assigned to SWAT team #4. One day, I returned from lunch, and the office was in an uproar. PG wanted a SWAT team of reporters dispatched to an AMTRAK derailment in Indiana, but two members of the assigned team, SWAT #2, were unavailable. McDonald quickly reassigned me and another reporter to SWAT #2. Reporters jokingly referred to the policy as Sure Hit Information Teams (SHIT).

There were endless stories of employees being fired for virtually nothing. At one point, the *Insider* composing room was complaining that the length of stories that were leaving the writer's desk weren't matching the space allocated in the layout. PG had laid down strict rules as to how margins should be set on typewriters to insure that story sizes met the layout's requirements and even threatened to have the margin adjustments on all typewriters welded at a specific point, so a meeting of the writers was called to determine the source of the problem.

At the meeting, he asked one of the writers what the blank sheet of page looked like.

"Oh, you know, Mr. Gallione," the writer replied with a facetious grin, "it looks like a plain, white sheet of paper." He drew an eight-and-a-half-by-eleven sheet with his forefingers in the air.

PG wasn't amused. Two weeks later, the writer was gone.

Since PG was an engineer, he kept close tabs on everything in the building, particularly the temperatures on hot August days. One day in late August of 1976, one of the writers opened the window at his desk to let in some fresh air. PG noticed that, for some reason, the temperature in the building had gone up two degrees. He sent McDonald out to determine why. McDonald returned and explained the cause. Without a moment's hesitation, PG thumbed down the writer with the death signal used by the ancient Romans in the Coliseum.

"He only opened a window," McDonald replied.

PG thumbed him down again and dismissed his executive editor. There were stories of secretaries who accidentally hit the wrong button during a telephone transfer to PG and were fired. A free-lancer was fired for wearing what PG referred to as a "clown shirt," which contained numerous, crazy colors. PG said it was "distracting" to other newsroom employees.

Thanks, PG!

One day in the summer of 1977, the entire gardening crew was fired after over-watering and killing the exotic powder-blue plumbago shrubs just outside PG's window.

Clive recalled the story about a tryout who, during his interview with PG, questioned the validity of UFOs.

"There's much more evidence that UFOs exist than evidence to the contrary," PG replied.

"I've never seen one," the tryout replied. "Do you expect me to believe that people from outer space are coming to earth in flying saucers to abduct human beings?"

"There are more things in heaven and earth than were ever dreamed of in your philosophy," PG replied.

The reporter appeared puzzled.

Apparently, the reporter didn't recognize the famous quote from Shakespeare's *Hamlet*. Needless to say, he didn't make his tryout.

The word "No!" wasn't in PG's vocabulary. Simon told the following story.

"Lucky" was a mongrel dog that had been saved from last-minute death at the Palm Beach County pound by the wife of an *Insider* editor; hence, the name. When the editor pitched the story to "the boss," he loved it and began to aggressively promote the loveable pooch's life with cute stories such as "Lucky Visits the Police Station" or "Lucky Goes Shopping." One afternoon, PG came up with the headline "Son of Lucky." The idea was to have Lucky impregnate some female dog and produce a story and photos of the proud father with his new son. Simon said, when the editor's wife who served as Lucky's handler was notified about the new lead, she said, "Oh, we can't do that. Lucky has been neutered."

When the information was reported back to PG, he replied, "Let's see if we can have his balls sewed back on."

*****

An integral part of PG's legend was his love of trains and editors had often heard him say, "Railroads built this country." On Tuesday and Thursday mornings, when the Florida Central train roared past *Insider* offices en route to Miami, PG would often venture out of his office and stand by the tracks to feel the train roar past.

"It's invigorating," he once told an editor.

One Tuesday morning, I was sitting in my cubicle when I heard the faraway whistle of the Florida Central locomotive and knew it was heading south. Moments later, I saw the side entrance to the "Inner Sanctum" open and PG, cigarette in hand, made his way across the grass to the railroad tracks. He looked up the tracks, saw the train approaching, and braced himself for the giant blast of air. As the giant locomotive blew past, he shivered momentarily, then smiled with satisfaction as he watched the railcars rumble past.

The greatest honor that could be bestowed on an *Insider* reporter was to be assigned a personal story for PG. The intellectual side of our Lord and Master was what intrigued me most. I couldn't reconcile the composition of a human mind which, on one hand, spent endless hours and millions of dollars creating mindless drivel for women, yet also had a keen interest in the great philosophical questions of the ages. How could one equate chewing gum and Aristotle? Somehow, in my mind, the two disciplines were mutually exclusive and left me searching for answers.

Finally, the job didn't come without its demons.

Many nights, I would sit at the bar at the Ambassador and wonder what in the hell I was doing spending my life "cooking" bland oatmeal for women. Every day, all around me, I watched talented, highly paid people running around wildly to create a stupid, mindless, ephemeral gossip magazine for a

Thanks, PG!

genius/madman. All of my energies and efforts were being wasted in the creation of meaningless fluff.

I quickly discovered I wasn't the only one tormented with such misgivings. One night at the bar, after a particularly bad day at the office, I saw a side of Simon I had never seen before. All that night, he'd been quiet, lost in his own thoughts.

"I'm going to resign tomorrow," he said finally. "I'm going in and tell PG I'm sick and tired of all the constant crap. It's driving me right round the bleeding twist."

Christ! I thought. *Simon can't quit.* I didn't want to have to learn a new editor.

"You're not really going to do it, are you?"

"Yes," he said. "I can't deal with it anymore."

"What would you do?"

"I've always had a dream of going back to the Lake District and opening a fishing shop. My wife and I could buy a cottage near Windermere. Maybe I can relax for a while."

"You're really going to do it?"

He nodded again, then paid his bar bill and quietly left.

Next morning, when I started to the office, I was filled with fear that Simon had resigned. The moment I entered the building, I glanced into his office. He was busy at work.

I stuck my head in the door.

"I thought you'd be in London by now."

He smiled and waved me off.

I turned to go.

"Hey, mate," he called.

I turned.

He offered his hand.

"I could never leave this madness," he said with a smile. "Where else could I have so much fun?"

I laughed.

"Now get out of here," he said. "I'm extremely busy."

Like Simon, I knew I could never leave the *Insider*. One of the greatest fears I'd had in my life was the fear of having to do the same, boring job day after day. I knew, at the *Insider*, I would never have to worry about being bored. The intrinsic madness of the place would never allow it to grow stale and routine, and, unlike all of the other jobs I'd had, the amount of money I was making was more than I could ever have dreamed. Even if it was mindless, stupid, shallow, and silly and served absolutely no obvious purpose, the alternatives weren't attractive. This was the pond into which I had set down my journalistic ducks and I knew that no matter how many misgivings I had, no matter how many demons I had to deal with, this was where I was destined to stay. I knew I had found my place.

Thanks, PG!

Chapter 7

Weird, Bizarre, and Unbelievable

The one thing I learned about the *Insider* early on was that it managed to push the boundaries of reality each and every day. PG was well aware that his readers had a strong sense of the mysterious, the paranormal, and the supernatural, and he gave them ample fodder in every edition.

"Truth is relative to the person who's telling it," PG said in one memo to his editors. "Everybody seems to have their own version of the 'truth.' Anytime you listen to an information provider, you're receiving the provider's own unique personal agenda. If you go to church, you get the minister's truth. At a political rally, you get the politician's agenda. Listen to a sales pitch and you get another 'truth.' There are as many different truths as there are people on this earth," the memo concluded.

Thus, over the years, especially in the late seventies and early eighties, I handled my fair share of weird, bizarre, and unbelievable stories.

One of my first assignments in this genre was "The Ghost of Cady's Cove." The lead sheet said the ghost of one Sadie Calhoun wandered around looking for her lover in the woods near Cady's Cove, a small town outside Meridian, Mississippi. The story was that, at the end of World War II, her long-time lover Horace was coming home to marry her. Her parents disapproved of Horace, so they planned to be secretly married. On the night she was to be married, Sadie, dressed in a white wedding gown and carrying a suitcase, walked to a nearby bridge to meet her future husband. As she waited, a pack of wild dogs charged out of the nearby woods and ripped her to pieces. Locals claimed that, since then, her ghost had been seen several times near the bridge, wandering in the night with a lantern and calling the name of her lover. My contact for the story was Verlon Carter, one of the locals who claimed he'd seen the ghost several times over the years.

"Come on over," he said when I talked to him on the phone. "We'll try to get a look at her."

Before I left, Simon said, "No matter what the locals say, you've got to have a credible source saying he believes the story and has seen the ghost. Otherwise, the story will never get into the paper."

"What qualifies as a credible source?" I asked.

"Usually, PG will only accept a police chief, a sheriff, or a mayor," he replied.

Two days later, I arrived at Cady's Cove, and met Verlon, a tall, bearded truck driver dressed in overalls. After darkness fell that night, we went to the bridge near Cady's Cove and waited in his pickup. I remember thinking that this was absolute madness. There was no such thing as ghosts, but I was determined to see it through.

After we had waited almost an hour, Verlon suddenly pointed into the darkness and blurted out, "There's Sadie."

In the darkness near the bridge, a light suddenly appeared. Then, as I watched, it started moving slowly toward us.

"Holy Christ!" I said in disbelief.

As the light moved nearer, I rolled down the pickup window. I could hear a woman's voice faintly calling, "Hooooorace, Hooooorace, Hoooorace."

I couldn't believe what I was hearing. We watched as the light moved closer and closer. Then, suddenly, the light continued moving, but the sounds stopped. For a full minute,

Thanks, PG!

there was no sound. Suddenly, it started again, and I heard the distinct, scratchy sound of a phonograph needle running amok on a vinyl record. I opened the door and got out of the pickup. Instantly, the light disappeared and the sound stopped.

"You scared her off," Verlon said. "She's gone now. She may not be back for another month or two."

As we drove back to town, I asked him who else had seen the ghost.

"Most of the folks around here have seen her at one time or another," he replied.

"Any public officials or people in high office seen her?"

"Deputy Sheriff Claude Rainey has seen her several times," Verlon replied. "We can stop and talk to him."

Some twenty minutes later, we stopped at the local sheriff's office. Claude, a balding, overweight man in his forties, was watching television. Verlon explained that I was a reporter and we had been down to Cady's Cove to see the ghost. I asked the deputy if he'd seen the ghost and believed the story.

The deputy looked first at me, then at Verlon, then back at me, and smiled from ear to ear.

"Sure! Sure!" he replied facetiously. "I've seen her lots of times and I believe the story is true."

I didn't reply at first. I knew he didn't believe it. He was just going along with the story to please Verlon, but I didn't say anything.

Verlon looked at me.

"There you have it," he said happily. "Straight from a deputy sheriff."

When the story appeared with the headline "*Insider* reporter confirms Ghost of Cady's Cove," there was a line drawing of a beautiful woman with long, dark hair dressed in a wedding gown wandering the night with a lantern.

The story got letters from readers all over the nation explaining that they had their own local ghosts and would be happy to work with an *Insider* reporter to prove their story. PG loved it! In my heart, I never did figure out where the light was coming from, but I knew the wailing sound was emanating from a recording device of some sort. It was definitely man-made. I never mentioned it. I had my story and everybody involved, especially PG, was happy. That was what mattered.

*****

Although I had known since childhood that I had some sort of extra sensory perception (ESP)—my grandmother called it "second sight"—I didn't broadcast it and, in fact, I was secretly afraid of it. PG, on the other hand, not only believed firmly in the powers of extra sensory perception, but he felt it could be scientifically proven.

Sources for these stories were always people who were well-known experts in the field. They had done research on paranormal phenomena, lectured and written books on the subject. One of PG's favorite ESP experts was an Israeli man named David Levine. In the spring of 1976, I was assigned to work with him on an experiment to prove the validity of ESP.

The experiment was to work like this. At a specific time on a specific date, David would concentrate on three specific images. Meanwhile, one hundred *Insider* readers were assigned to concentrate hard at the specified time and date, then call in to the *Insider* and reveal what images they were thinking of at the exact same time and date as David.

Once the experiment was complete, David revealed that he had been thinking about a dog, a tree, and a book. When I canvassed *Insider* readers, forty-one of them had imagined a dog and a tree while only thirteen had imagined a book.

Thanks, PG!

Although the three images were common, when one considers the odds of 54 out of 100 people having the same thoughts as David when compared to all of trillions of thoughts the human mind is capable of, the statistical probability is simply mind-boggling.

Predictions from so-called *Insider* "psychics" were a staple at the paper. PG said he wanted to satisfy the "women's intuition" in his readers, and he always welcomed the latest predictions from the publication's so-called psychic experts. Qualities required to be an *Insider* psychic were imagination, a knowledge of show business and current events, as well as some inkling of what PG required for publication. The stories themselves were wacky, silly prognostications relating to the subjects that appeared regularly in the *Insider*.

In creating a predictions story, ten psychics would be assigned to ten reporters. The reporters often referred to the psychics as "psychos," and they would contact their assigned psychics and provide hints as to what PG wanted. Once psychics returned their predictions, these would be written by reporters and forwarded to editors, who chose the best fits for PG's requirements.

I did many, many prediction stories in the early eighties. Of all the stories one could handle for the *Insider*, the prediction stories were the most fun, but also the most stupid. The ultimate effect of a prediction story was to forecast a happier, healthier, more hopeful life for readers. After reading a prediction story, the reader should feel inspired and more secure about his or her life.

These stories were formularized and followed a set of general rules that guaranteed successful prediction stories. Following is the set of rules for successful prediction stories and an example of implementing each rule. All of the examples are from the year 1983.

***A famous star will have a real-life experience similar to a recent film or TV show he or she starred in. For example, after Farrah Fawcett stars in a film about battered wives, she will open a home for abused women in Los Angeles.

***Fans' wildest suspicions about some famous star comes true. Singer Boy George, famous for his colorful and garish costumes, will reveal under hypnosis that he was an Egyptian Queen in another life.

***Something tragic will happen to an enemy of the USA. Hated Libyan dictator Muammar Gaddafi will be stabbed to death by one of his thirteen wives.

***New technologies will make life easier. Scientists will invent a powerful new laser that would clear snow-covered streets instantly, making winter driving safer than ever.

***A prediction will confirm the existence of ESP, UFOs, or some paranormal experience. The space shuttle will retrieve space debris that confirms the existence of UFOs.

The above five principles were the essential template for creating prediction stories decade after decade at the *Insider*. All that changed in the above format was the characters and the events on the world stage. Once a reporter had done so many prediction stories, one got a pretty good idea of how *Insider* history repeated itself.

Another PG favorite was miraculous survival stories. The *Insider* had hundreds of these type of stories in inventory, but they were never published unless the victim said, "I saw my life flash before my eyes." That was the single line PG wanted for such a story.

Once, I was assigned a story about an Alaskan woman who had been severely mauled by a grizzly bear during a camping trip. When I first filed the story, I quoted her as saying, "The bear tore my ear off with its claw."

When Simon saw the copy, he said, "Oh no, she's got to say, 'The savage beast ripped my ear off with a single blow.'"

Thanks, PG!

"That's kind of overdramatic," I replied.

"Insider readers love overdramatic," he said. "Reality is so boring. We've got to add some color. Also, you've got to get her to say, 'I saw my life flash before my eyes.'"

"She might not say that," I protested.

"Remember, you can ask the question, 'Did you see your life flash before your eyes?' and if she says, 'Yes,' you can quote her as saying that."

When I called her back, I asked, "Did the savage beast rip off your ear with a single blow?"

"Oh yes," she said. "My ear went flying into the air."

"Did your life flash before your eyes?"

"Oh yes," she said again. "I thought I was a goner."

*****

There was a broad range of innocuous, self-help stories reporters referred to as "Get an Expert" stories. These stories were designed to support a headline like "How to Cope with People Who Try to Put You Down," "Why Superstitions Are Good for You," or "The Best Time of Day to Make a Decision." Sources for these stories were almost always psychologists at a major university and the *Insider* always had a list of anywhere from twenty to fifty psychologists for such stories. They were usually paid $150 to $200 per story.

First, the reporter would call the psychologist, provide the angle, and offer hints as to what they were expected to say. For instance, if the headline was "Why Superstitions Are Good for You," the reporter might hint that "superstitions broaden one's sense of wonder" or "superstitions are healthy because they provide entertainment and take you beyond boring reality." Almost always, the psychologist would have some original reasons to support the headline. Once the psychologist called back with his replies, the story was written in Insiderese and read back to the psychologist for his approval. I never had a single psychologist disagree with the finished story. Reporters referred to the psychologists as "trained seals."

Sometimes, stories bordered on the truly comical. I was once assigned a story about an Arkansas farmer who claimed to have been struck by lightning twelve times.

"I know it's far out there," Simon said, "but if he's credible and a respectable member of his community, PG will publish it."

Hollis Whisenant was a tall, sunburned man in his late fifties who had spent his life working the land. When I shook his hand, the first thing I noticed was a big scar on the right side of his face.

"I got that," Hollis said, indicating the scar, "when I was thirteen years old."

Hollis said he was riding in a horse-drawn wagon filled with corn when the incident occurred.

"I could see the storm coming when I headed across the field," he said. "Suddenly, there was a loud boom and a blinding light that came out of nowhere. That's all I remember. I was knocked out of the wagon and into a drainage ditch. When I woke up, I had this big gash on my face and there was blood all over the place. My daddy found me and carried me to the hospital. They sewed me up, but the horse was killed dead."

He produced a photo of a demolished wagon and a dead horse lying on its side, its teeth flared in pain and its hair burned to a crisp from the voltage of the strike.

Another time, he said he was drawing water from a well when lightning struck the metal chain attached to the bucket.

"For just a minute, I could feel the tingle of the electricity running through me like when you accidentally stick your

Thanks, PG!

finger in a light socket," he said. "I thought I was a dead man that time."

Hollis said he'd also been struck while fishing, while visiting his aunt, and still another time at church.

"Can you imagine God sending down lightning on a man while he's at church?" Hollis said. "There's something dead wrong with that."

Hollis said every time he saw rain approaching, he stopped whatever he was doing, went inside, and closed all of the windows and doors.

"Ain't no word for how lucky I been," he said. "Next time will be thirteen. They say it's an unlucky number."

The local sheriff said, "I wasn't there during all the times Hollis says he was struck by lightning, but I've always known him to be an honest man. He's worked his farm, paid his bills, and gone to church with his family on Sunday. You can't ask much more of a man than that."

With the sheriff's recommendation, PG approved the story.

When the story was published, the headline read "Lighting does strike twice! Ask Hollis Whisenant!" An accompanying photo depicted Hollis looking fearfully toward a dark sky.

Since the *Insider* had a regular UFO editor, I only did one UFO story during my entire career there. I traveled to Kalispell, Montana to interview Wendell and Doris Thompson. This is their story.

Late one night, the couple was returning from a hunting trip in the Glacier National Forest near their home. It had been a successful trip. They had taken two elks and picked more than two bushels of chicken of the woods mushrooms. Suddenly, as they rounded a bend on the road, they saw a brightly lit object blocking the road ahead of them and stopped.

"I didn't know what in hell was going on," Wendell said. "It was eleven p.m. and this thing lit up the night like it was broad daylight. It was round like a Frisbee, and there was a warm heat coming from it. I wasn't as afraid as I was curious."

Wendell said he and his wife emerged from the pickup and stared at the shining, round object.

"As we stood there looking at this thing, a beam of light was put on us. It started out a light blue color, then slowly turned to green, and I started getting sleepy. That's all we remember. When we woke up, everything was gone and we were left standing on the side of the road butt-naked."

"Naked?"

"Yeah," he continued. "The truck, the two elk, the mushrooms, my new hunting rifle, and all of our clothes were gone."

"What happened?"

Wendell shrugged. "I guess they took everything with them," he replied. "I hated it about that new hunting rifle. I paid over six hundred dollars for that thing. I guess it's gone to wherever that thing come from. Mars or outer space or wherever."

Wendell said that if a park ranger hadn't come along and picked them up, they could have frozen to death without clothes in the cold Montana night.

I stared at him incredulously. He knew I didn't believe him.

"I swear to God, it's true," Wendell said, crossing himself.

It all sounded hokey to me. I decided to talk to the sheriff.

Bitterroot County Sheriff Ross Gilmore, an overweight, all-business, bespectacled man in his sixties, produced a photo of the couple taken by the park ranger. They were huddled under a blanket the ranger had given them, trying to cover their modesty as best they could.

"That's the way the ranger found them," the sheriff said. "From all the evidence, they're telling the truth. Even down to the burn marks on the edge of the road. Me and a deputy went out there the following morning and, sure enough, you could

Thanks, PG!

see where grass on the side of the road was dead from some source of intense heat."

"What do you think happened?"

"I don't have a clue," he said. "I don't believe in flying saucers or little men from outer space, but I just don't know what happened."

"Did you find the truck?"

"It's been four months and nothing has turned up."

"It didn't disappear into thin air," I said.

"I agree," the sheriff said, "but I don't have an answer."

*****

For more than five years, PG went through what reporters called his "World Records" period. During that time, he was obsessed with the world's records on all of the extreme attributes of human anatomy. These subjects included the person who was tallest, shortest, fattest, thinnest, oldest, the one with the most teeth, the largest hands, the biggest nose, longest fingernails, and on and on.

These human oddities quickly opened the floodgates to an even longer string of world record stories designed especially for *Insider* readers. There was the dog with the longest tongue, the celebrity with the most wives, the biggest pet, the largest feet, the biggest cake, the fastest eater, most pierced, most tattooed, etc. Reading these stories was like wandering into a carnival sideshow.

Invariably, the photos were the meat of the stories. It was one thing to describe in words a man with thirty-eight-inch fingernails, but it was a totally different experience when one views the photo and watches the curling fingernails wind down and down, finally to the tip. I think PG probably spent a lot of time on Coney Island as a youngster viewing the odd and unusual. Although he proudly tried to show the world the

William Randolph Hearst side of himself, the P.T. Barnum side was alive and well.

The British reporters called this phase PG's "Extremes Period."

Thanks, PG!

Chapter 8

President Carter

As a child growing up in the hills of North Alabama, I had seen movies and TV shows where the main character lived in the concrete canyons of a big city, wore tailor-made suits, traveled everywhere in taxis, and frequented exclusive restaurants and entertainment venues with a beautiful woman on his arm. As a child, I never dreamed I would ever have such an experience, but thanks to PG, I lived that life in spades.

*****

By the end of 1976, Watergate had paralyzed the government and Americans were ready for a change in leadership. Tricky Dick was so consumed with defending himself about his role in the Watergate mess that the government was basically running itself. The Republicans knew that, with Nixon's VP as their candidate, they were holding the short straw in the upcoming election. Their candidate was not only part of the establishment voters had learned to hate, but he had pardoned his infamous predecessor for his crimes. As a result, he had a certain amount of the same stink as his predecessor.

Meanwhile, the Democrats, taking advantage of the voters' mood, sought out a candidate that was as far removed as possible from Washington and the Watergate scandal. They wanted a candidate who not only presented a fresh face, but projected a wholesome image of the so-called "common man." Finally, after intense screening, they selected a Southerner, a man named James Earl Carter Jr. who, with his toothy grin and impressive record as governor of Georgia, seemed to fill the bill. The choice proved to be a wise one and, in the general election on November 2, 1976, Carter won by a landslide victory.

In late November, three weeks after the election, Simon called me into his office.

"Do you fancy a trip to Washington?" he asked.

"Got a government waste story?"

"No," he replied. "I mean permanently."

I drew back. "Permanently?"

He nodded. "The boss wants you to go. Now that we've got a Southerner in the White House, he says 'the tall guy from Tennessee' is the person to cover him."

It was so sudden, I didn't know how to answer at first.

"You'll be working out of the Washington bureau," he said. "There will be government waste and some medical stories. Mostly what he wants are personal stories about the new president."

"Can I think about it?" I asked finally.

There was a long silence.

"You want to go up there for a few days just to see if you like it?" Simon suggested. "You can go sightseeing, check out the bureau, get a feel for the place. It'll be totally different from south Florida."

I told Simon to have the travel department set up the trip.

The next morning, I caught a flight from Palm Beach to Washington National. Before I arrived, I knew exactly what my plans were. I had always wanted to go sightseeing in the nation's capital. As soon as I checked into the DuPont Plaza Hotel, I caught a taxi and went straight to the Smithsonian.

Thanks, PG!

There, I spent four hours seeing the Spirit of St. Louis, replicas of the Columbian ships, the wooly mammoths, and the seemingly endless collection of art and artifacts housed in the museum. It was too much for one day.

That afternoon, I visited the *Insider* bureau at 14th and Constitution, and as I walked through the shiny, marble hallways, I passed offices representing newspapers from throughout the world. There were publications from Hong Kong, Jakarta, Sydney, Berlin, Vienna, Amsterdam, Moscow, New Delhi, Johannesburg, and Rio de Janeiro. *My goodness,* I thought, *this is the big time*. Afterward, on a trip to Capitol Hill, I wandered through the congress and senate chambers, soaking up their history. Finally, I lazed away the rest of the autumn afternoon in the park at DuPont Circle, listening and watching as the locals argued politics and played chess.

Everything in this town centered on the government. It was filled with history, culture, music, theater, and the arts and, whether I wanted to admit it or not, I was becoming weary of Florida. I still loved the beach and I liked to go deep sea fishing every month or two, but culturally, Florida didn't have much to offer. I had never lived in the middle of a large metropolitan city and, secretly, I had always wanted to live the life of a full-fledged city boy and wear suits, dine at fancy restaurants, and go to the theater with a beautiful woman on my arm. As big cities go, it wasn't New York, but it was close. Suddenly, I realized how I hungered for the different and the new. The following morning, I called Simon and told him I wanted to make the move.

Two weeks later, I was safely ensconced in the Hilton at the top of Connecticut Avenue and had my first assignment, "The Childhood of Jimmy Carter."

"There has got to be some scandal in this man's life," Simon said. "All little boys tie cans to dog's tails and tear wings off butterflies. PG wants to know all of the bad things he's done. The clips say he's had lots of problems with his younger brother over the years. Be sure to check that out."

So I joined a team of reporters and off we went to Plains, Georgia, Carter's hometown, to see what we could dig up. The oldest of four children born to James Earl Carter Sr. and the former Lillian Gordy, the new president was part of a second-generation peanut farming family. From the first day of the investigation, "Jim Bob," as Simon facetiously nicknamed the new president, seemed to be a model citizen. As a high school student, he was class valedictorian, a member of the FFA, and an avid churchgoer. After high school, his father used his political connections to win him an appointment to the Naval Academy at Annapolis, where he graduated with honors.

After completing his service in the Navy, Carter returned to Plains for several years and ran the family farm before entering politics. Quickly, he moved up the ranks, becoming first a state senator, then, after one unsuccessful bid, he was elected governor. He brought a toothy smile, a down-home folksiness, and a certain childlike innocence to Georgia politics. At the time he was elected president, he'd been married to his high school sweetheart, the former Rosalynn Smith, for twenty-eight years and they had three adult sons and a young daughter.

"Jim Bob's" mother, Miss Lillian, was the family matriarch and obviously on my short list for an in-depth interview.

When I sat down with her at the "Pond House" near the family home, the first thing she asked was my affiliation.

"The *National Insider*?" she said. "Oh, Billy Don, I love your publication. There are great recipes and household tips, and I can catch up on all the Hollywood gossip, but I could never be seen buying one. Why, I'd be the laughing stock of Plains, Georgia."

"So how do you get it?" I asked.

Thanks, PG!

"Thelma Blevins gets it in the mail," she replied, almost in a whisper. "Once she reads it, she gives it to me. Once I've read it, I pass it on to Henrietta Cline and she passes it to Rhoda McElroy. Is all that stuff true about UFOs and aliens?"

"There lots of evidence to support it," I replied. "Whether it's true or not, people like to read about it."

"Oh, yes!" she replied. "It's all very interesting."

I asked about the long-time rivalry between Jimmy and his brother Billy.

"When they were young, they were the best of friends," she said. "Although there was several years' difference in their ages, they played ball, fished in the creeks, and worked on the farm together. After my husband died and Jimmy returned and took over the family business, Billy was sorely disappointed. He thought the farm should come to him after my husband passed and, from that point on, nothing was ever the same. If Jimmy said something was black, Billy called it white."

Miss Lillian said her oldest son had inherited the gift of gab from his father and it had carried him a long way in life.

"Jimmy could talk to people," she said. "He could convince people to do things and get them to take orders from him. Billy, on the other hand, never had that. He liked to keep to himself and read books."

After eight days in Plains, we found none of the bad things PG had been expecting. The new president had been a model citizen. He'd never been arrested, and he'd been an avid churchgoer who followed all the rules and proved to be an asset to his community. The only bad thing we found was that, once, during the church service when he was eight years old, he'd taken a penny out of the plate when it was passed.

"Is that all you've got?" Simon asked when I filed the story.

"That's it," I said. "This guy is squeaky clean."

I could hear the disappointment in his silence.

John Isaac Jones
*****

On the plane from Atlanta back to the nation's capital, I met a tall, shapely brunette who had been vacationing with her parents in Savannah. From the first moment I looked into her brown eyes, Diana Kincaid could make me smile. She had a confident, easy-going intelligence, and her long hair flounced about recklessly when she laughed. A native of Richmond, she worked as a tour guide at the Manassas National Battlefield in northern Virginia. When we parted at baggage claim, she gave me her number.

I settled into covering the new president. I knew PG had no interest in politics. *Insider* readers couldn't care less about the infighting between the Democrats and Republicans. Subjects like budget deficits, foreign policy, cabinet reshuffles, and Supreme Court appointments were totally lost on *Insider* readers. What PG wanted was personal tidbits about the president, his idiosyncrasies, anything unusual about him and his pets, his sense of fashion, and quirky, silly gossip overlooked in the daily press.

Early on, I learned that stories about his brother Billy were almost as popular as stories about the president himself. One afternoon, I got a call from the mayor of Plains, saying Billy had bought a new home in nearby Buena Vista.

"Now that his brother is president, Billy thinks he's too good to live in Plains with us regular folks," the mayor said. "Well, I can tell you, the people of Plains are just as good as Billy Carter."

Outraged, he went on and on.

"The people of Plains won't miss him," the mayor said. "If he's so high and mighty, he can just go to Buena Vista and stay there. The people of Plains are glad to be rid of him."

Thanks, PG!

The call was a gift from heaven. It went on the front page and more than made up for the poor showing I had on the childhood story.

A few days later, there was a truly stupid story with a headline that read, "Nation's capital welcomes southerners." PG wanted to be sure that his readers knew Carter and his new administration of mostly southerners were being graciously welcomed in the capital. The story consisted of quotes from long-time Washington residents saying things like "President Carter is going to make us a fine president," "We just love southerners here in the nation's capital," and "I've never seen such fine people as these southerners who are here to help our new president." *Great God,* I thought, as I filed the story, *what am I doing with my life?*

Two weeks after my return from Plains, I contacted Diana and she agreed to drive up to DC and spend the following Saturday with me. The minute I saw her walking down Constitution Avenue to meet me at the National Press Building, I remembered how much I had liked her.

"I hope you didn't pay the ransom," she said offhandedly as I hugged her.

"No," I replied with a big smile. "They wouldn't accept a check."

We both burst out laughing.

Over lunch on Capitol Hill, we discussed the Battle of Chancellorsville and the ingenious tactics Lee and Jackson used to outflank Hooker and the Union troops and turn what appeared to be a loss into a major victory.

"Lee's tactics at Chancellorsville would rival anything ever attempted by Napoleon or Patton," she said. "His troop movements during that battle were God-like."

This woman knew and loved the history of the American Civil War as much as I.

After lunch, we went to a small bookstore on Connecticut Avenue so she could buy a birthday gift for her mother. Finally, we ended up in Georgetown browsing the boutiques, gift shops, and restaurants, and generally enjoying one another's company. That night, we attended a performance of *Hamlet* at the Shakespearean theater next door to the Supreme Court. She had two glasses of wine during intermission and was more than a bit tipsy when we left.

"Alas, poor Yorick," she kept saying to a make-believe skull as we got into the taxi. "I knew him well, Horatio. A fellow of infinite jest, of most excellent fancy: he hath borne me on his back a thousand times."

Then she would erupt in girlish giggles.

The driver looked back at us.

"Is she okay?" he asked.

"She's fine," I replied.

We engaged in some light foreplay as the taxicab made its way back down to Constitution Avenue.

"Your car is still in the underground parking at the press building," I reminded.

"I'm not going back to Virginia tonight," she said. "You know where a girl can find a room?"

I smiled.

Before she left Sunday morning, she invited me to come down to Manassas the following weekend and promised a personal tour of the battlefield. I asked if it was true that overconfident Yankee civilians actually spread out lunches on the battlefield to watch their troops rout the Confederates.

"Yes," she replied. "And I can take you to the exact spot where they spread out, then hurriedly had to pack everything up as the Confederates swept through the Yankee lines."

I knew I would be spending many weekends with this woman.

Thanks, PG!
*****

Another of my regular chores was to attend the Ninth Street Baptist Church in Washington, the First Family's adopted church, and report on the president's worship activities. On Sunday mornings, I would arrive around 9:15 a.m. and drive slowly past the front entrance. At either corner of the block, I would see the Secret Service agents at their posts. All of the old women and other parishioners would be loitering near the front door, waiting to greet the First Family.

Around 9:45 a.m., the presidential limousine would pull up in front and Jimmy, Rosalynn, and little Amy would emerge. Striding beside the president was the marine corporal who carried the "football," the briefcase that contained the secret codes for launching the nation's nuclear weapons. Once the trio had run the gauntlet of well-wishers, they would enter the church and take a seat in their special pew. The First Family pew was situated perfectly in the middle balcony of the upper level in the church facing the pulpit. Once everyone was seated, the minister would begin the day's sermon and, after some thirty minutes, he would begin to call on churchgoers to testify for Christ.

Invariably, the pastor would call on the president, and Jimmy would launch into a lengthy diatribe about the influence Christ had had on his life. Once the president started talking, it was almost like he was delivering a political speech, but, in this case, he wasn't asking for votes; he was making his personal testimony for Jesus. Once services were finished, the First Family had to run the gauntlet again to return to the presidential limo.

Over the next few years, I branched out from President Carter stories and wrote FDA whistleblower, self-help, quirky history, and more government waste stories than I care to remember. There were fluffy little pieces about Miss Lillian's favorite soap operas and Rosalynn's favorite dresses and little Amy taking her dog to the vet.

PG was keenly interested in the president's health and, every few months, Simon instructed me to go to the White House and get all of the results from the president's most recent medical checkup. The White House physician, a balding, serious man in his early sixties, would always meet me in a small press office near the front door, then he would read off the president's test results on blood pressure, PSA, dietary requirements, cardiac indicators, and sodium levels. Even if all of the tests were good, PG felt it was worth a story because he wanted his readers to know their president was in great health.

Even before he was elected, Carter was the object of his younger brother's revenge. When the press met Carter's family in Plains for the first time, Billy was ready to pounce.

"My whole family is crazy," he said. "My mother joined the Peace Corps when she was sixty-eight. My sister is a motorcycle freak, my other sister is a Holy Roller evangelist, and my brother thinks he's going to be president. I'm the only sane member of this family."

After riding his brother's coattails to fame as a good ole beer-drinking country boy, Billy got an agent, became a regular on the national talk show circuit, and even had a beer named after him. While promoting Billy Beer in London, the younger brother relieved himself in the bushes at Heathrow Airport in front of the press and a host of international dignitaries. Naturally, the world press had a field day with that one.

In July 1980, at a time when Iranian militants were holding more than six hundred Americans hostage, Billy registered as a foreign agent of the Libyan government and admitted to receiving a $220,000 "loan" for facilitating oil sales from the renegade nation. Of course, the president had to respond.

Thanks, PG!

"I'm deeply concerned that Billy has received funds from Libya and that he may be under obligation to Libya. These facts will govern my relationship with Billy as long as I'm president. Billy has had no influence on U.S. policy or actions concerning Libya in the past, and he'll have no influence in the future," said a White House statement.

In late 1980, while the president was fighting an uphill battle for re-election, his chief advisor remarked, "This damn Billy stuff is killing us."

Meanwhile, I loved my life in DC. After work each day, I would leave the office, take the subway to DuPont Circle, then walk to the Hilton. Once I had showered, I would take my bicycle and explore off-the-beaten-path historical sites such as the Georgetown restaurant where JFK proposed to Jackie, the apartment where Senator Grover Cleveland housed his mistress and their illegitimate child, or the boarding house where John Wilkes Booth and his accomplices laid plans to assassinate Lincoln.

One of the true wonders of the nation's capital has always been its history. Raw history lives in every square inch of Washington, D.C., but one must go out and discover it. Many times, the act of discovery will prove to be more entertaining that the history itself. During those history-seeking afternoons, if the mood struck, I would stop by a French restaurant on Connecticut for a red wine and bouillabaisse, or pedal down to Georgetown for coconut chicken at the Tsingtao on Wisconsin Ave.

On weekends, if I was in town, Diana would drive up from Virginia and we would dress up and attend a Broadway play at the Kennedy Center or a performance by the Washington Metropolitan Symphony. We rubbed elbows with international diplomats, congressmen, senators, famous doctors, and lawyers. Little theater was Diana's favorite venue, and we would often attend performances of *Waiting for Godot* and

Death of a Salesman played by smaller, out-of-the-way theatrical groups.

Like me, Diana could ramble on endlessly about Civil War battles, the generals, the strategies, the casualties, and the impact of a particular battle on the overall war. She could discuss Pickett's famous charge at Gettysburg just as eloquently as she detailed the tragedy of the wounded Union soldiers who were burned alive at the Battle of the Wilderness. As a lover, she was soft, gentle, silly, and giggly, and had this delicious, off-handed wit, which would erupt at the most unexpected moment. Sometimes, a man can be with a woman and, out of nowhere and for no logical reason, the whole world opens up. Diana was that kind of woman.

I spent four glorious years in the nation's capital. Wearing tailor-made suits, tipping cab drivers with ten-dollar bills, waiting in line with famous lawyers, doctors, politicians, and world diplomats, eating at expensive restaurants with names like Bombay Holiday, Tiberio's, and Acacia, and attending the Kennedy Center theater to see a Broadway play or a musical were the stuff of which my dreams were made. I would return to Rosebud after President Carter's term, but I would forever remember the days I played the full-fledged city boy in the nation's capital. PG had not only provided the venue, but the money for my escapades.

Thanks, PG!

Chapter 9

Last Days of Elvis

One afternoon in early June of 1977, I had just walked into the *Insider* offices in Washington, D.C. when the bureau chief said, "Call Simon! Now! It's urgent!"

I picked up the phone.

"Get on the next plane for Rosebud!" Simon said frantically. "Urgent! Urgent! Be in the office tomorrow at nine sharp. Whatever it takes, be here!"

"What's going on?"

"It's a secret story," he replied. "Just be here tomorrow!"

The next morning when I appeared at the office, he immediately took me into a conference room and closed the door.

"Elvis is in a high-class drying out facility in Minnesota," he said. "The boss wants you to check in as a recovering alcoholic to get the story. He says since you're from Tennessee, you might even get an interview with him. Company will pay for everything to get you inside. Go in there as a patient and see what he's doing there."

An hour later, I had all of the papers from the business office to get me admitted to Brookwood Manor, an exclusive drug rehab facility near Minneapolis-St. Paul. Once I returned, Simon instructed me to talk to Jim Northrop, a long-time *Insider* editor who, as a recovering alcoholic, had been a former "patient" in such facilities.

"You want to put on a good show," Jim said. "Be drunk when you get there. They'll run medical checks on you and you want your triglyceride count to be high so you'll be believable. Have some booze in your suitcase because they'll confiscate it upon arrival. Also, have several prefabricated stories ready attesting to your struggle with alcohol over the years. You'll be expected to share those with other patients."

The following morning, I was on a plane bound for Brookwood Manor to begin my stint as a recovering alcoholic. When I changed planes in Chicago, I went into the airport bar and had three martinis and a bloody Mary. Upon arrival in the twin cities, I was greeted by a smiling, curly-haired young man wearing glasses. Finally, the other patients and I were assembled and he loaded us and our luggage into a station wagon and started the drive to the facility.

Brookwood Manor was a sprawling, spotless, yellow-brick facility designed to calm the mind and rest the spirit. Nestled snugly into the side of a mountain, the buildings cascaded gently down the green foothills to a clear, turquoise lake on the valley floor. Each patient's room looked out on a natural, terraced palette of deep blues and rich greens. Recreational facilities included a par-three golf course, tennis courts, a full-sized basketball court, and a fully equipped gym. As I got out of the station wagon and started to the admissions building, I thought facetiously, *A place fit for a king.*

Inside the admissions office, I showed them my papers. I told them I had a landscaping business in Washington and had been an alcoholic for the past eight years. After a bevy of psychological and physical tests, I was assigned a room and allowed to roam the grounds as an official alcoholic. As instructed, I had a pint of vodka and a half-bottle of scotch in my luggage when I arrived. A staffer searched my luggage and confiscated both bottles while I slept.

Thanks, PG!

My roommate was a burly, middle-aged man from Detroit named Frank who said he was in for an addiction to flavored vodka. He owned a restaurant that served drinks, so he had easy access to his favorite forms of alcohol. Likable, talkative, and good-natured, Frank said he "knew the ropes" and would be happy to help me learn the place.

Brookwood Manor was like a hospital more than anything else. Nurses in crisp, light-blue uniforms wearing stethoscopes around their necks manned the stations on each floor. The dining hall, which reminded me of a college mess hall, served excellent, generous portions. There was a separate program for women, and the only time the men saw the women was in the dining hall. Many of the men would feign hunger to go to the dining hall simply to see and talk to the women.

Everywhere one looked—in the dining hall, the dorm rooms, even the bathrooms— there were framed photos and plaques shouting the twelve-step motto, "God, grant me the serenity to accept the things I cannot change, the courage to change the things I can, and the wisdom to know the difference."

Although the patients were there to receive help for their addictions, many bragged openly about their exploits with drugs. Oscar, a consumptive, balding man in his late fifties who never smiled, proudly proclaimed that he'd been in detox a total of 169 times.

"That's a record, far as I know," Oscar said.

"Oh, no," said Jeff, a long-time counselor. "The record is held by a lawyer from Seattle who was in detox a total of 214 times."

I could see that Oscar was miffed at being upstaged by the counselor.

Every evening, all of the patients would gather in the recreation room around 5:30 to watch television until it was time for the evening meal. Of course, drugs and their abuse was never far from everyone's mind, and quite often the constancy of the subject became the butt of jokes.

One evening, all of the patients were quietly assembled watching the evening news when the announcer said, "Recent studies have shown that the high concentration of nitrites, which are used as preservatives in bacon, can cause stomach cancer, high blood pressure, and heart disease."

Immediately, someone in the crowd quipped, "All you guys who have been shooting bacon are in a lot of trouble."

Instantly, the entire assemblage erupted in raucous laughter.

After I had been in for three days, Frank invited me to play golf on the par-three course. We had played two holes and I was putting on the third. Then, out of the blue, Frank said, "You know Elvis Presley is here."

My heart skipped a beat. I tried not to look too excited.

"No," I replied innocently. "I didn't know."

"He's got a private room with a male nurse," Frank continued. "Some evenings, he'll come out and watch TV and talk with us before we go eat. Elvis and I have become pretty good friends."

"Any idea when he'll be back?" I asked.

"Probably tonight," Frank said. "Usually on Wednesdays, he'll come and watch television."

I acknowledged his statement, trying not to appear too interested, although my heart was racing with excitement.

That night, I was waiting with Frank and the others in the recreation room at 5:30. Around 5:37, a late comer announced that Elvis was coming down the hall.

Moments later, when Elvis and his male nurse rounded the corner and entered the recreation room, I was shocked. Somehow, I had expected to see the thin, handsome, dashing man with the rakish smile and the leering eye I had seen so many times in movies, television, and magazines. The man

Thanks, PG!

who appeared before me was anything but that. Dressed in pajamas and bedroom slippers, he was a far cry from the handsome, youthful, energetic Elvis I had imagined. Grossly overweight with a beer belly, he was bent over like a seventy-year-old, and his steps were slow and deliberate. His chin and jowls were severely bloated, and his eyes were glassy and dull.

As Elvis entered, his eyes scanned the room and immediately fell on Frank. He smiled and made a beeline for us.

"Frank, how's it going," Elvis said, taking a seat directly across from us. "Who's your friend?"

"I want you to meet Billy Don Johnson," Frank said. "He's from Tennessee."

"Hi, Billy Don," Elvis said, offering his hand. "What part of Tennessee you from?"

"Gatlinburg," I lied.

His lips pursed in approval.

"I been to Gatlinburg a few times," he said, his eyes lighting up with a twinkle. "They got lots of pretty girls back in those mountains. I know. I've been there."

He paused. Everybody was quiet and waited for the King to speak.

"In the early seventies, must have been '71 or '72, I met this little brunette named Debbie."

He stopped.

"No, maybe her name was Amanda," he continued. "You know, after a while, you meet so many women you can't remember their names. You remember what color her hair was, but you don't remember her name. Funny how those things work. Anyway, her father ran a hardware store in Gatlinburg. Oh, she was a sweet little thing. Me and her slipped away for a weekend at her uncle's mountain cabin. I spent some wonderful nights in her arms."

Elvis grew quiet.

"Bet you been with lots of women," one of the men ventured.

Elvis smiled faintly. "Yeah, I've been lucky about that," he said. "Some guys can't get a woman; me, I have to fight them off."

"You're the king," one man ventured.

"Yeah, I guess so," he said almost apologetically. "But all of that's over now. I haven't got long for this earth. I'm headed downhill now. You know, life is like going up and down a hill."

He raised his hand to indicate the incline of a hill.

"When you're born, you go up and up and up until you reach forty," he said. "Then it's all downhill. That's where I am now."

"Elvis, don't say that!" Frank said. "You're got a lot more living to do."

Elvis forced a smile. "That's nice to say," he replied. "But that's not the way it is. I always knew I'd die young. It wasn't meant to be any other way."

He stopped.

"Now don't get me wrong," he said. "I'm not afraid to die. I've had a good life. I just miss my mama so much. Not a day passes that I don't miss her. I'm ready to go be with my mama again."

There were more than thirty men in the room, but everyone was enthralled. The King was holding court and you could hear a pin drop.

Finally, Elvis took a deep breath, then looked over at his nurse.

"Charley," he said. "I changed my mind about dinner. I'm tired. I think I'll go back to the room. I want to rest."

Instantly, the male nurse was at his side. Once he was on his feet, Elvis turned.

Thanks, PG!

"Enjoyed talking to you fellows," he said. "I'll see you again."

Me, Frank, and the others said our good-byes.

As I watched Elvis slowly trudge out of the rec room with the help of the male nurse, my mind was flooded with memories of my Uncle Dee. When I was growing up, I had an uncle named "Dee." His birth name was Dee Ledrick, but everybody called him "Dee." He was my mother's youngest brother and had always been pampered by the women in his life. Although he had two older sisters, everybody in the family knew that my grandmother worshipped her only son. "Dee is the light of my life," she would say and the daughters, probably to appease their mother, supported her psychotic love for her son. When he started smoking at age twelve, my mother and her younger sister would steal eggs to buy cigarettes for him. My Uncle Dee was a man who grew up expecting women to please him.

As an adult, he was a tall, handsome man who traveled throughout the South working as a welder on construction projects. Early on, he showed a special knack for winning women and having his way with them. Very proud of his sexual conquests, he would say gleefully, "Why buy a cow when you can get milk and butter through the fence."

When my grandmother died suddenly in 1968, he was absolutely devastated. He couldn't work for more than two weeks, and he spent days drinking and telling his friends about how much he missed his mother.

The last time I saw him alive was in the spring of 1974, a full year before I went to work for the *Insider*. He had a heart condition, the result of alcohol, the interminable, all-night romps with his women, and the stress of traveling. When I entered the hospital room and saw him sleeping in the bed, I hardly recognized him. All of the dash and devil-may-care energy that had been his trademark as a young man were gone now. His face and jowls were bloated and dark, puffy pockets had collected under his eyes, his movements were slow and deliberate. He was a shell of the fun-loving, devil-may-care rake I had known as a child.

Two months later, as he was dying of a heart attack, his final words to the nurse who was administering CPR, were, "Tell Mama I love her."

During the years I knew him, I had heard him tell the story of how life is like climbing a hill at least a dozen times. In my mind, I suddenly realized that Elvis' life had been a virtual duplicate of my Uncle Dee's.

Over the next two weeks, I saw Elvis one other time. On that occasion, he was sullen and withdrawn and, after some ten minutes of watching television, the male nurse announced that Elvis had decided to eat in his room. As the nurse started back to the room with his charge, one of the patients, a tall, debilitated man named Ernest from Arkansas said Elvis had promised to sign his memory book. The male nurse took the book and told Ernest the King would sign and return it later. Two days later, the memory book was returned and we received the news that Elvis had checked out.

On that news, I announced to the institution's staff that I was abandoning my rehabilitation efforts. They pleaded and argued that I needed further help, that I hadn't dented the surface of their program, and, if I didn't get help at Brookwood, I would spend the remainder of my life "in a bottle." Tired of arguing, I left the executive's office, packed my bags, returned to Rosebud, and filed my story.

"ELVIS IN DRUG REHAB!!" that week's new edition shouted. "*Insider* Reporter goes undercover for details!" "The King's Final Days!"

When I saw the new edition on the stands, I knew PG would be happy. I had done my job.

Thanks, PG!
*****

Six weeks later, Elvis died while sitting on the commode. The prolonged use of prescription drugs had enlarged his colon to the point that he could no longer defecate. What an inglorious end for the world-famous entertainer who single-handedly paved the road for all of the rock and roll greats of the future! His body was discovered by his girlfriend and the news swept the world.

After the announcement that morning, I joined a team of *Insider* reporters on a flight to Memphis. Simon asked that I be part of the team because I was friends with Elvis' stepmother. I had interviewed her and her sons several times in the past on Elvis stories. In Memphis, we bought up everybody in sight for exclusive stories. There was the old black woman who had cooked deep-fried banana and peanut butter sandwiches for Elvis. We bought his gardener, his chauffeur, two housekeepers, various family members, close friends, and several long-time business associates.

The *Insider* paid one of his cousins $18,000 to get a photo of Elvis in his coffin. A miniature camera hidden in a cap with a remote shutter release was used. The photo appeared on the front page and, not only was the issue the best-selling *Insider* edition of all time, but it drew livid consternation from the mainstream press. As usual, it was pure jealousy. In London, during a convenience store robbery that week, the thieves made off with not only all of the cash, but all of the *Insider* copies as well.

Of course, situations like this always led to some hanky-panky at the *Insider*. A week after Elvis' death, I was sitting in the office working on a story when the police came in. They went straight to one of the long-time editors, an Englishman named Oliver Williams, and announced he was under arrest. When he stood, the officers frisked him, told him he was under arrest, and placed cuffs on his wrists. Immediately, the editor fainted and the officers were obliged to physically carry him out of the office. Later, we learned that the editor had conspired with two other reporters and a photographer to sell the photo of Elvis in his casket to an overseas media outlet for the manufacture of tee shirts. They reportedly were to receive $50,000 for the photo. Of course, all involved were summarily fired.

As I look back now at the tragic ends of Elvis and my Uncle Dee, I see endless similarities. Both were undisciplined, self-indulgent country boys with hearts of gold who only wanted to work, have their women and their drugs, and live their lives happily ever after. Both loved to give impromptu gifts, shied away from conflicts, and had no interest in the great philosophical or intellectual pursuits of the day. Both had an unnatural, obsessive love for their mother.

Elvis' obsession with his mother is well documented, and some sources have claimed that the great singer slept in his mother's bed, and she in his, until his early teens. Whether this is true or not will remain a secret of history, but one point is very clear. The psychotic love both men had for their mothers prevented them from having a normal, stable relationship with another woman. My uncle never had a guitar in his hand, but Elvis never had a welding torch in his, yet, as human beings, both were cut from the same identical cloth. My Uncle Dee lived from 1932 until 1974. Elvis lived from 1935 to 1977. Both men died at age forty-two. Like Elvis, my Uncle Dee was buried beside his mother as requested. Also, like Elvis, he wanted to spend eternity beside the only woman he ever truly loved.

Thanks, PG!

Chapter 10

Governor Wallace in Love

For more than thirty years, Governor George C. Wallace of Alabama spoke out against racial integration in America. After realizing he was helpless to stop it, he apologized to black people, said he was wrong to stand in the schoolhouse door, said he was wrong to deny them their civil rights, and asked for their love and forgiveness. When he died in 1998, he represented the last political whimper of the old segregationist southern ways.

A native of Clio, Alabama, he got the nickname "Fighting Little Judge" after he proved himself a capable bantamweight boxer in high school. After graduating with a law degree at the University of Alabama, he launched straight into politics and, after winning a state senator's race, he ran for the Alabama governorship for the first time in 1958. In those days, every political race had a Negro plank and each candidate had to state his position on race. During that first race, Wallace lost to a state senator who was backed by the KKK. After the election, Wallace said he lost because he was "outn*******d" by his opponent and he vowed that it would never happen again.

Thereafter, his political philosophy took on a firm segregationist theme and, over the years, that philosophy was solidified to the point that on January 4, 1963, when he took his first oath of office as Alabama governor, he uttered the now infamous words "Segregation now, segregation tomorrow, segregation forever."

In the 1966 governor's race, Wallace was unable to succeed himself as a result of term limits and ran his wife, Lurleen, as a proxy. She easily beat her opponent, but after holding office for only two years, she died of uterine cancer in 1968 and Albert Brewer, the lieutenant governor, assumed the duties of the office. He ran against Wallace in 1970. It was during this campaign, when I was a reporter for the *Hamilton Courier*, that I met Wallace for the first time.

One Saturday afternoon, Arthur Ray Shaw, the *Courier's* city editor, and I attended a political rally in the parking lot of a local shopping center to hear Wallace speak. Some 12,000 to 15,000 local supporters were in attendance. The governor already knew Arthur Ray as a member of the press since he had covered Wallace's campaign during the first gubernatorial race. As Wallace spoke to the deeply partisan crowd, his eyes fell on the two of us.

"Don't believe any of the lies you read in the *Hamilton Courier*," he said with a snarl, pointing down to Arthur Ray and me. "All they want to do is sell you newspapers and make you believe I'm not the best governor this state has ever had."

Suddenly, the crowd glared hatefully and moved away from us. Many of these people were supposed to be our "friends," but one polarizing word from the governor and we became enemies.

The single thing I remember was the savage snarl that formed on Wallace's face when he made the statement. His face screwed up like a mad dog that had suddenly become angry and was prepared to do harm to anyone or anything who opposed him. It was then that I recognized what extraordinary power he could have over an audience. Later that month, he won another term.

Thanks, PG!
*****

A year later, as a single man, he began secretly courting the beautiful Cornelia Ellis Snively, the niece of former Alabama Governor Jim Folsom. She was the same winsome teenager I and other members of my junior high school class had seen at the governor's mansion during our 1957 class trip. Tall and statuesque with a sultry brunette beauty, Cornelia had been a performer in a Florida water-skiing show, liked fast racecars, and once toured with the famous Roy Acuff as a country music singer. The press later nicknamed her "the Jackie Kennedy of the rednecks." They were married in January of 1971.

In the fall of 1971, Wallace called a meeting of Governors John Bell Williams of Mississippi, Lester Maddox of Georgia, and himself on the tarmac of the Montgomery airport and explained that he felt one of them should run in the upcoming presidential primary on a segregationist ticket.

Maddox explained that, of the three, Wallace had the best name recognition.

"You'll have a better chance of winning than either of us," he said.

Williams agreed.

So, sensing that there remained some appeal to his segregationist message in the North, Wallace took his new wife and his message north of the Mason-Dixon Line. The "Fighting Little Judge" was going north to promote a principle that had been defeated more than one hundred years earlier when Gen. Robert E. Lee surrendered at Appomattox courthouse. It was as if Wallace was trying to roll back the nation's history.

Of course, once the campaign began, the press dogged Cornelia about her role.

"Oh, I just walk along at his side and look pretty and wave to the crowds," she said. "At the end of the day, I provide the emotional response he needs when he gets lonely. And he does get lonely after a tiring day of making speeches and shaking hands."

Cornelia, who was nineteen years younger than her husband, continued, "Sometimes, he thinks I'm like a little toy doll and he can just pull my string and I'll say or do anything he likes. Really, I'm not that way, but I go along with it because he's my husband."

A full two weeks before the primary began, Wallace told a friend, "Somebody's going to get killed before this primary is over, and I hope it's not me."

The moment he started campaigning in Maryland, he realized he was in dangerous territory. In Hagerstown, police had to be called in after young whites and blacks disrupted his speech. As Wallace left a rally the following week in Frederick, a brick came out of nowhere and crashed into his chest. Later the same day, students at the University of Maryland threw ice cream at him and, in a Wheaton shopping center north of Washington, rotten tomatoes came flying out of the crowd and stained his shirt blood red. It was an ominous sign.

The following day, as Wallace made his way through a crowd of supporters at a Laurel Shopping center, a failed young drifter named Arthur Bremer poked a snub-nosed pistol through a crowd of onlookers and fired five shots point blank into Wallace's body. Wallace instantly collapsed backward on the shopping center asphalt and, as security personnel wrestled the gunman to the ground, Cornelia threw her body over her husband's prostate form, staining her white dress with his blood.

Wallace, although pale from shock and blood loss, never lost consciousness. That night, at a Silver Spring Hospital, a

Thanks, PG!

doctor issued the grim prognosis. Four of the five bullets from Bremer's gun had not caused life-threatening damage and could be removed, but the fifth had lodged in his fluid-filled spinal canal and would cause severe nerve damage. That night, Wallace reported that he had no feelings in his legs and, when released from the hospital several days later, he was in a wheelchair.

Back in Montgomery, Cornelia told the press that she and the governor were "getting by" with their new situation. With teary eyes and a cracking voice, Cornelia said she and the governor would fight on and proclaimed their determination to recover from his injuries.

Over the next few years, the governor quietly continued his gubernatorial duties in a wheelchair and, in 1974, easily won reelection. Three years later, rumors swirled that the governor and Cornelia were having marital problems. There were stories that she had had his telephone in the governor's mansion bugged. The governor accused her of infidelity and some state capital sources said they heard shouting matches in the governor's mansion in the wee hours. Finally, the governor filed for divorce and that was when I became involved.

*****

In the spring of 1978, I was still working in Washington when I got a call from Simon.

"Governor Wallace and his beautiful young wife are getting a divorce," Simon said. "Word is she is having an affair with another man. PG says you're the only one that can get the story."

So I was paired with another reporter, an older Englishman named Harry Longmuir, to go to Montgomery, Alabama and see what we could dig up. Once we arrived, we set about trying to find contacts. Three years earlier, when I worked in

Birmingham, I had several inside contacts in the state capital, but, after calling them, I started to hit a brick wall. A former state senator from Sylacauga said he couldn't say anything because "if it got back to the governor, I'd be finished politically." A former state investigator who I knew during the sheriff Walton investigation, said, "The governor is a very vengeful man," and also refused to talk.

In my hometown of Hamilton, I had known several political enemies of the governor, but all had been out of the loop for several years. In short, I was getting nowhere. Finally, I decided to call Ron Jacobs, the fellow *Age-Herald* reporter I had been arrested with three years earlier.

When he answered the phone, I explained my assignment and asked if he could help me with some sources. I could hear the hesitancy in his voice.

"Do you think I would help you on a story like that?" he said self-righteously. "Sex and sensationalism have no place in respectable journalism."

"The tabloids aren't what you think," I said.

"You're working for a trash magazine," he said. "Those people wouldn't recognize the truth if it hit 'em in the ass."

There was a long silence.

"What if I could get you a check for one thousand dollars to provide me the names of some credible sources?"

"You're crazy!" he shot back. "That's checkbook journalism. Don't you know that when you pay for information, that information is tainted?"

Now I could feel my own anger rising.

"The information is not tainted," I said. "It is rendered truer."

Another silence.

"I've lost all respect for you, Billy Don," he said finally. "You've reneged on all of your journalistic principles. You're a prostitute, a whore."

Thanks, PG!

There was a long silence.

"Look," I replied, "I'm here to get a story, not discuss journalistic principles."

"You have no journalistic principles when you work for a publication like the *Insider*," he said. "Nobody believes any of it."

"Ron," I said, "you've got it all wrong."

There was a long silence. Although we had been close friends three years earlier, now we were far apart.

"There is no way I am going to help you," he said finally.

Another long silence.

"Good bye!" he said, then suddenly, he hung up the phone.

When I heard the click, I burst out laughing. I wasn't sure why, but I felt a certain righteousness within my soul.

So I was back to zero again.

That night, as I lay in bed, my conversation with Ron came back to my mind. Thank God, I had been lucky enough to escape the very trap that he was reveling in. His journalistic life still consisted of police reports, tornadoes, county commission fights, biggest pumpkin contests, endless political feuds, and ten million city council meetings. PG had saved me from that dreary existence. Over the past three years, I had grown into a larger, more dynamic reporter while Ron had remained the same. As always, he was still in pursuit of his beloved Pulitzer Prize. When I went to sleep that night, I was giddy with happiness at my good fortune.

The following morning, the Englishman and I were at our wit's end. I had exhausted my contacts and didn't know where to turn. Then we got a call from Simon.

"Cornelia's mother did the New York talk show circuit this morning," he said. "She didn't say a whole lot, but she's going to be in Montgomery this afternoon. Let's try for an interview."

I knew this was our last chance. If we didn't get something from Cornelia's mother, we would have to go back to Rosebud empty-handed.

That afternoon, Harry and I met "Big Ruby" Folsom at the Montgomery airport. She was tall, a full six feet, very animated, and wearing a black flamenco dancer's outfit complete with the traditional black, round-brimmed hat and bangles. We introduced ourselves and explained our mission. She explained that she would be staying at the same hotel we were in.

"What do you want to know?" she asked as we rode in the taxi to the hotel.

"We want to know if it's true Cornelia has been seeing other men," I replied. "Why are they getting a divorce? What's the source of their problems?"

"That's a lot of information," she replied. "You know if I told you all that, Cornelia would kill me."

So the Englishman and I set about wining and dining "Big Ruby" to get her to talk. We had drinks at the hotel bar, then went to an Italian restaurant where she had chicken Alfredo, au gratin potatoes, and three slices of cherry pie. Then we returned to the bar for more drinks. All the while, Harry and I were pressuring her for information and she kept resisting. My God, this woman could drink some booze.

Around ten p.m., Harry, after the heavy Italian food and more than his share of drinks, decided to turn in.

"We're not going to get anything from her," he said. "She's a lost cause."

"Go on to bed," I said. "I'm going to try one more time."

"Good luck," he replied and went up to his room to bed.

When I returned to the bar, Big Ruby was watching the bar television. I could see she was very drunk. We made small talk about the television show, then she turned and put her hand on my knee.

Thanks, PG!

"Billy Don, you know, you're a good-looking man," she said, rubbing my inner thigh. "When I get tight, I like to have some sex."

I didn't answer.

She moved closer to me.

"Would you be interested in something like that?" she said, continuing to stroke my inner thigh.

I didn't answer at first. I knew this was my last chance.

"Will you tell me all about the governor and Cornelia's marital problems?"

She smiled.

"Only if you're good...."

An hour later, back in her hotel room, "Big Ruby" and I did a sit-down interview.

"Talk about little man syndrome," she started. "This guy took the cake. All that little squirt ever cared about was politics. He would get up in front of big crowds and talk about how he loved God and family and the Bible and all that, but all he ever loved was politics. Being in front of crowds made him feel bigger than he really was and he loved it."

I could sense there was no love lost between the governor and his mother-in-law.

"After Lurleen died, he come nosing around Cornelia," she said. "He was afraid to meet her in public because of all the publicity, so he would come and court her at my house. He would call and say, 'I'm going to drop by for just a few minutes' and he would stay for several hours."

Although they spent several nights together before they were married, "Big Ruby" said that Cornelia confessed they didn't have sex until after the ceremony.

"Cornelia used to tell me what a prude he was in the bedroom," she recalled. "He refused to let her run around the bedroom naked; she always had to wear a robe. And before they went out in public, he always checked to be sure her dress wasn't too short.

"That was the real 'Fighting Little Judge.' Prim and proper and prudish. Cornelia used the word 'Victorian' to describe him."

She suddenly burst out laughing at the sound of the word.

"Victorian," she said again. "Yeah, Victorian is probably the right word for him. Like in the days of bustles and bowler hats and mustaches and horse-drawn carriages."

She burst out laughing again at the thought.

"After he was shot, he couldn't do anything in the bedroom," she said. "My daughter is a natural born woman. She needs a man to bring out the woman in her and he couldn't do anything."

Although there were rumors of several different men, "Big Ruby" said there was basically only one.

"That was the construction engineer in Eufaula," she said. "Cornelia really liked him. He had lots of money and he liked to fish and so did she.

"In his entire life, the only thing he ever loved was political power. And he would use anything and everything—his wife and kids, his dogs, whatever he needed—to gain it. He would have sacrificed his own mother for political gain."

When I left her room that night, I had the story I wanted. The next morning, I told Harry what had happened during the night. After the three of us had breakfast at the hotel restaurant, we said our good-byes, and Harry and I caught the first plane back to Rosebud.

On the plane, the Englishman turned to me. "You'd do anything to get a story, wouldn't you?"

I looked at him.

"Of course," I said. "I work for PG."

Thanks, PG!

Chapter 11

Hollywood Bound

By the late summer of 1985, I had been a reporter with the *Insider* for ten years. Four of those years, I had spent in the Washington bureau during the Carter Administration, and for the remaining six, I had been based in Rosebud. During that time, I had covered/written every major story category the magazine offered except celebrity stories. I had traveled all over Europe, been to South America three times, twice to the Middle East, once to Russia and North Africa, and traversed the USA, Canada, and Mexico more times than I cared to remember. I had consolidated my talents as a tabloid reporter.

During those ten years, the publication had changed. It was now printed in color, and the content of the stories had moved away from the bizarre and the weird toward a more realistic, friendlier timbre. There were fewer stories about UFOs, ESP, and the unbelievable, and more stories about self-improvement, household tips, wacky, historical tales, quirky stories about famous people, and many inspirational stories like brave cop, good Samaritan, rags to riches, honest person, "Why I Love America," success without college, and "Will you please try to find a home for little Harold?"

It should be noted that PG had turned fifty-eight in January of that year and was still going strong. Although he still smoked two packs a day and remain cloistered in the "Inner Sanctum," staffers would still occasionally see him venture out to the railroad tracks to feel the blast of the Florida Central train as it roared past.

There had been changes in company infrastructure. The accounting department had hired a feisty young South African to monitor expense accounts, meal allowances in New York had been raised to one hundred dollars per day, and all interviews had to be taped and vetted by the new research department. PG had inaugurated the spectacular "World's Biggest Christmas Tree" event in Rosebud every Christmas. So far as PG's essential genius, it remained solidly intact, circulation was soaring, and the publication was making millions.

*****

In the mid-to-late eighties, American journalism went through an incredible revolution. This was when information became "data" and newspapers throughout the world began the top-to-bottom integration of computers into the total publishing process. During that period, the storage, manipulation, and composition of information underwent a revolutionary change as "data" moved from paper to computer hard drives. Reporters no longer traveled with portable typewriters; they carried laptop computers and used word processing software to compose their stories.

Even further and more importantly, reporters no longer pored over pages upon pages of paper documents to gather information for their stories. They simply entered a search string and searched a database. This not only revolutionized the retrieval of data by making it much easier, but it made all sorts of information instantly available that had been extremely elusive in the past. Suddenly, specialty information such as property and vital information data that would have required days upon days to retrieve in the past were now

Thanks, PG!

available in seconds. The very essence of the reporter's trade had drastically changed.

PG had started converting the *Insider*'s editorial department to digital in late 1984. All portable typewriters were handed in to the business department, and on each reporter's desk sat a shiny new computer monitor, keyboard, and mouse. On trips, reporters carried laptops and each reporter was responsible for knowing how to efficiently use both the laptop and the desktop and manage the data between them.

One afternoon in late July, Simon called me into his office.

"There's going to be a purge next week," he said. "There are 2,823 stories in inventory, and PG is going to fire two editors and five, maybe six, reporters."

"Am I on the list?"

"No," he said, "but your name was mentioned in the discussion."

"In what context?"

"PG wants you to become an editor," he said.

I froze at his words.

"Oh God, I can't do that," I replied finally. "I could never do that."

"Why not?"

I hesitated, trying to find the words. "If I had to go in and face PG every day, I'd be a lunatic by the end of the first week."

He stared at me with disbelief. "Why?"

"He does something to me," I replied. "When I'm around him, I'm scared to death of him. I can't explain it. I can't even look in his eyes."

Simon smiled. "He has a spell on you?" he said, almost making a joke.

"It's serious to me," I replied defensively. "Call it whatever you like, but I can tell you now I could never go in and face PG every day. That's like looking into the eyes of God."

There was a long silence as he peered at me.

Suddenly, he burst out in hysterical laughter, and then just as suddenly, he was calm again.

"I know what you mean," he said. "I get that feeling sometimes myself. He's a powerful human being. Okay," he said. "I don't know what I can do to prevent it. You know PG gets what he wants no matter who it hurts."

"I know," I said. "That's what I'm afraid of."

Another long silence.

"You could take off sick for a few days. That would give us more time."

I didn't answer.

"Let me see what I can do," he said finally. "We have until Friday of next week."

I turned to go, then quickly turned back to him.

"There's no way I can be an editor," I said again. "No way!"

When I left Simon's office, I couldn't imagine what I would do if I got fired at the *Insider*. It would be sheer hell for me to have to work for a large metropolitan daily again. The *Insider* had become my life.

On both Thursday and Friday mornings of that week, I asked Simon if he'd heard anything. No news, he said. I was getting nervous. The following Monday morning when I arrived for work, Simon called me into his office. I feared the words he was about to say.

"As you know, everything about this place is in a constant state of madness," he said. "I don't see how this place gets from Monday to Tuesday. Nothing, absolutely nothing is ever as it seems."

"I've grown to expect that," I replied. "What else is new?"

Thanks, PG!

"There are only 282 stories in inventory, not the 2,823 originally reported," he said. "The girl entered the data wrong in the database."

"What about the purge?"

"Only one editor and three reporters are getting the axe."

"And what about me?"

"PG still wants you to be an editor."

"Holy Christ," I said. "I guess I'm dead meat."

For the next three days, I was on pins and needles. I dreaded even seeing Simon because I was afraid I would hear the worst. Then, late on Wednesday night, he called.

"Are you sitting down?" he asked.

"Yeah, what's up?"

"I think I have a solution to your problem."

"Come on, talk to me."

"You want to work in LA?"

"Work in LA?" I replied. "What happened?"

Simon explained that, on Wednesday, Charlotte Kimble, the employee in the computer room who entered the data wrong, was fired. Her long-time boyfriend, who had been working temporarily as a reporter in LA decided, in that case, he was returning to Florida so they could be married.

"This means I don't have a reporter in LA," he said. "Do you want to be my new reporter in LA?"

I heaved a sigh of relief. At least I had an escape route now.

"PG doesn't want me to be an editor anymore?"

"Already asked him," Simon said. "A new reporter in LA is top priority."

I was suddenly ecstatic. I could face LA any day before I could PG.

"Give me a night to sleep on it," I replied.

"I have to know in the morning," he said.

When I hung up the phone, I knew the decision had been made. I remembered nine years earlier when I moved from Florida to Washington and how, with that decision, I didn't realize it, but I hungered for the different and the new. It was deja vu. I could feel myself at the same crossroads again. I wasn't unfamiliar with Los Angeles. In 1964, after I left Auburn, my friend Jim Baines and I had wandered out there and spent six months living hand-to-mouth. I liked LA. There was a different set of attitudes out there. The next morning, I called Simon and told him I would make the move.

*****

So the little old redneck white boy from north Alabama went to Tinseltown to be a reporter. I was afraid at first. I had heard other reporters talk about how hard it was to work in LA, how hard it was to find leads and reliable sources, and how every celebrity story was vetted over and over by the lawyers, and if a story got hit with a libel suit and they won, you were dead meat.

On the other hand, I believed in myself. I had confidence in the investigative skills I had learned in Birmingham. I knew that down deep I had some great digging skills. I was just not sure how I was going to use those skills in Hollywood.

In Los Angeles, the *National Insider* offices were located in Suite 812 at 8300 Sunset Boulevard in West Hollywood. The building was an unassuming light green and yellow structure that housed all manner of people involved in show business. There were publicists, lawyers, agents, attorneys, producers, guild offices, production companies, film editors, sound and recording groups, and other unnamable spin-offs of the entertainment industry too numerous to mention.

Of all the tenants in the building, it was the stars' publicists who were the rudest, the most downright mean toward *Insider*

Thanks, PG!

staffers. In Hollywood, publicists serve as image-makers to the stars and their job is to keep their clients' reputations as squeaky clean as possible. They were well aware that the occupants of Suite 812 were out to learn all of the personal secrets of their clients. They knew we were digging up items like who their clients were sleeping with, what drugs they were using, and what projects they were in or planned to be in. As a result, they hated us.

Once one was identified as an *Insider* staffer, publicists would go out of their way to annoy, embarrass, or downright insult that person. They would intentionally bump into staffers in the hallway. Another ploy was to slam the door in one's face as they were coming out of the men's room. Since the *Insider* office had a buzzer, which required identification before entry, the publicists and their minions loved to ring the buzzer, then disappear.

Early on in Hollywood, one learned that money talks. Hollywood had always been full of wannabe actors, producers, directors etc. who were living hand-to-mouth or waiting tables, hoping to be discovered. As a result, there were always plenty of people who would provide information in return for the almighty dollar. All information that was paid for was thoroughly checked out before the source was paid. A reporter didn't take information and immediately publish it because the source seemed credible. The information from each and every source had to dovetail with the information the reporter was receiving from other sources; otherwise, it would never get past the lawyers.

I learned that the easiest to approach and most accessible group of knowledgeable people in Hollywood were the gay guys that hung around the stars—young and old. There was no part of show business that didn't employ several gay men as assistants, wardrobe or hair and makeup people. Not only were they knowledgeable, they loved to gossip, and, even better, loved to gossip when they were getting paid.

So, once a week, I would run an ad in *The Advocate*, largest newspaper for the LGBT community, which read: "Got a celebrity connection? If so, tabloid reporter will pay big bucks for provable information" with my phone number.

Many of the calls I received were dead ends. The information was either secondhand or old, or so vague it was virtually unprovable. However, probably twenty percent of the calls provided leads that resulted in stories and, sometimes, blockbuster stories. There was a synergy between story leads and contacts and understanding this synergy was key. If one had a new story lead, one had a potential new source. If one had a new source, one potentially had new leads. Understanding and knowing how to exploit that synergy was critical to success as a Hollywood reporter.

If one wanted to witness what endless money, sex, and drugs can do to a person, Hollywood provided a front-row seat. It was a seething cauldron of insatiable lust, drugs, big money, and egomania. Finally and foremost, it was the world's primary pathway to the ultimate titillation of one's nerve endings. The legend of sin in Tinseltown has never come close to its stark reality. The reality has always been much larger and more flagrant than its mythology. Also, it has to be the most interesting topic any reporter could ever cover.

From a legal standpoint, Hollywood stories were a totally different animal as tabloid stories go. When I was an investigator in Birmingham, we had one attorney who vetted potentially libelous stories before publication. At the *Insider*, there were three. In other words, everything in the article that was potentially libelous had to be backed up with hard, substantiating evidence. It never ceased to amaze me that most people believed *Insider* gossip stories were fabricated fairy tales. Anyone with any intelligence should know one can't

Thanks, PG!

print a story about a married man sneaking around with a mistress without being sued. An *Insider* reporter could play fast and free with stories about UFOs, ESP, and ghosts, but celebrity stories, like medical stories, had to be locked up tight.

*****

I couldn't write this book without mentioning Neal...or "Notorious Neal," as he was lovingly renamed by a couple of British reporters visiting the office. Neal was an early-thirties, openly gay man, and very handsome. He was obsessed with Marilyn Monroe and old Hollywood stars in general. A self-described country boy, he had written a book called *Nashville Babylon*, a tome about sex and sin in the country music industry. Affable, witty, and extremely intelligent, Neal was probably the greatest Hollywood reporter who ever lived.

I considered myself a good reporter, but Neal was a magician. I was a good digger. I could find sources and gather, assimilate, and organize facts to the point where I could draw good conclusions. Neal, on the other hand, was an absolute master at getting inside under disguise. It was breathtakingly beautiful to see him in action. Once, when the story broke that a major celebrity had been hospitalized at Cedars-Sinai, I called the hospital and asked about the condition of Mr. Johnson. I received the response "Fred or Robert Johnson?" At that point, I had the name of a patient to visit, which gave me access to the hospital corridors.

Two hours later, as I started into the hospital, I saw Neal going in ahead of me. He was wearing an official-looking deliveryman's outfit and had a bouquet of flowers in hand. I watched as he approached the visitor's desk, explained his mission, and obtained a visitor's pass. Neal filed the story that afternoon.

Another time, there was a charity bash at a Beverly Hills Hotel and several major stars were in attendance. I couldn't gain access into the private party, but I did sneak into an adjacent empty conference room and peeked inside. As my eyes scoured the room, I saw Neal. He was dressed as a waiter, passing around champagne to the guests. Another time, I saw him gingerly sliding down the side of a hill, wearing white tie and tails, into the backyard of a secluded mansion in the Hollywood Hills where a posh celebrity wedding was being held. Those of us who had managed to be looking in from the empty mansion next door that we had managed to rent for the day from the caretaker were incredulous as Neal just brushed his suit lightly and joined the rest of the servers at the wedding.

In the early spring of 1992, Neal contracted AIDS from his long-time partner who came from a well-to-do family in the Northeast. After his partner was unfaithful, Neal was diagnosed with a highly virulent strain of HIV.

"How am I going to tell the company I've got AIDS?" Neal asked me. "I can't just call my editor and say, 'Hey, good morning. I've got AIDS.'"

"Knowing you," I replied, "you'll come up with something."

Three weeks later, there was a clipping from the *Advocate* on the office bulletin board. The headline read, "How I contracted AIDS." Neal's byline appeared under the headline with an accompanying photo. By the end of the day, everybody in the bureau knew about Neal's condition.

Neal died in the fall of 1994. In early August, the doctors said he had only a few days to live and his parents came to say their final farewells. They remained in LA a week, waiting for him to die, but after death refused to cooperate, they finally decided to return home. Three days after they returned home, Neal passed away quietly in his sleep. Neal Hitchens was one of the kindest, wittiest, smartest, most affable human beings I

Thanks, PG!

had known in my entire life. I loved Neal. What an amazing human being! If all people were like Neal, what a wonderful world it would be!

*****

Working celebrity stories required patience and instinct. Many hours would be spent on stakeouts, watching a celebrity's home, or sitting in a restaurant or bar waiting for a star or a star's lover to appear. Quickly, one learned the value of waiters, valet parking employees, hostesses, cab drivers, strippers, parking lot attendants, and others who were in a position to witness the comings and goings of major stars.

Lower echelon employees in show business, people who could share information without fear of losing their jobs, were also valuable. These included grips, production company truck drivers, line producers, extras, freelance makeup artists, and sound people. Employed actors, actresses, directors, and producers simply would not divulge the secrets of other employed actors, actresses, directors, and producers. Hospital sources were best for leads about celebrities who were hospitalized, but they were difficult to acquire because, if hospital authorities learned about their shenanigans, they were immediately fired.

Celebrity weddings were a staple at the *Insider*, especially weddings between two major stars. Invariably, security was tight and, as a tabloid reporter, one had to work around the edges to get information. Photos were extremely important for weddings, so helicopters were often involved. Many times, if a wedding was being held outside, a photographer with a telephoto lens in a helicopter could get some great photos.

On the other hand, there were often problems. Once, when an *Insider* helicopter got so close to the wedding ceremony that the blades wash blew away the bride's veil, the groom blasted the belly of the chopper with a shotgun. Many times at weddings, we would put flyers on wedding-goers' car windshields telling them we would pay big money for information and photos. It would surprise one how many responses we received.

Many celebs would hold weddings away from LA to avoid the tabloids. Carmel, Sausalito, and Napa Valley were favorite locales. Once, during a wedding in Carmel, Neal and I nailed the story and photos by hiding in a tree not more than fifty feet from the ceremony.

If PG decided that he wanted to reveal the ending of a television episode before it actually aired, we would be required to buy a script. Usually, the easiest way to buy a script was from someone lower on the production company totem pole. This was almost always a grip, script girl, an extra, a line producer, or some low-ranking member of the show who had access to scripts, but wouldn't question what the buyer were going to do with it. Many times, script girls would slip a script to their boyfriend/husband and have them deliver the product and collect the money. Usually, the *Insider* paid one thousand dollars for a script.

Sometimes, the show producers themselves used to leak us the final script, especially when a show was in trouble and they wanted to attract attention to the "cliffhanger." More than one in trouble TV series would offer inside gossip in order to get publicity for the show, usually with excellent results because of the huge readership of the *Insider*.

Buying a movie script was much harder than buying a TV script, especially if the project was not shooting in LA. Once, I bought a script for a movie being shot in Canada and we paid five thousand dollars, but it was rare that PG would ask for a movie script.

PG was well aware of the speed at which digitalization was pervading the entire publishing industry and used this

Thanks, PG!

revolution to his advantage in Hollywood. In downtown LA, PG had purchased a data processing company. This was a company used by bill collectors, private investigators, and attorneys to locate hard-to-find people; in this case, Hollywood celebrities. Since major celebrities knew tabloid reporters were constantly on their heels, they did all they could to evade discovery.

For instance, they never listed the address of their private home on public records. They always used a P.O. box or their agent's office address or even a fictitious address. Through the data processing company, *Insider* reporters could instantly locate the private address and phone number of virtually anyone.

"Big stars can hide their dalliances from their wives and friends," Neal would say, "but there's no escaping PG."

This was so true.

In the late eighties and early nineties, massive amounts of information were being lifted, both legally and illegally, from public databases. Hackers were gathering public information such as voters lists, vehicle and motorcycle tag numbers, boat registration information, and birth, marriage, and divorce records almost at will and selling them to news outlets.

There was one CD called "America First," which contained the Los Angeles County Voters lists complete with names, addresses, phone numbers, and occupations that *Insider* reporters had as early as 1993. When the OJ trial began in 1995, *Insider* reporters followed the sheriff's van, which transported jurors to and from the courtroom to the jury parking area. Once we had the jurors' tag numbers, we simply cross-referenced those with the names on the voters list and had the names of all twelve OJ jurors and alternates only a few weeks into the trial. It was safe to say that PG had well prepared his troops to do battle on the Hollywood front lines.

Ultimately, I would spend ten years in the Hollywood bureau.

Thanks, PG!

Chapter 12
Hollywood Stories I

Brando

As a tabloid reporter in Hollywood, you have a front row seat to witness the effects Tinseltown has on the human animal. You witness first-hand the dehumanizing effects that stardom has on their personal lives. In some cases, superstars become so caught up in their own mythology they seem to forget they were ever human. They not only become puppets of the industry, but puppets of themselves as they play out the roles of big Hollywood stars that fans expect. After a while, they start to believe that life offers nothing more than being a Hollywood star. This is the story of a man who spent many years in that trap, then discovered what was truly valuable.

Marlon Brando was often called the "greatest actor who ever lived." He became a major star at twenty-eight after bursting on the screen in a string of hugely successful and critically acclaimed films about the New York waterfront, a motorcycle gang, a Mexican outlaw, and a famous mutiny. He won his first Academy Award in 1954 at the age of thirty for the film *On the Waterfront*. Not only did he have the title role in *The Godfather*, the most famous mafia movie ever made, but he also had a leading role in *Apocalypse Now*, the most famous Vietnam War movie.

As a Lothario in Hollywood, Brando had a history of wives and lovers that was the stuff of legend. Every film project he undertook seemed to bring a new wife or lover. Business meetings in London and Paris consistently produced a new round of one-night stands and weekend liaisons in Cannes and Monte Carlo. His taste ran for exotic, sultry women. His first wife and mother of his oldest son, Christian, was a sultry Indian actress that he quickly divorced after learning her Indian background was not real. She was followed by a Mexican and a Tahitian woman. Toward the end of his life, he publicly acknowledged a total of eleven children, three of whom were adopted, but one biographer claims he may have fathered as many as fifteen offspring.

In the early summer of 1988, Simon called me late one afternoon.

"Marlon Brando has got his maid pregnant and has bought a home in the Valley for her," he said. "PG wants a love nest story. He wants photos of them together in the love nest."

"It's going to take some digging," I replied.

"That's what you're good at," Simon said. "Get going!"

Moments later, I was on the phone with Melody, an on-then-off-again girlfriend of Brando's son, Christian. Melody had been a regular at Brando's Mulholland home for parties and social visits for many years and always had access to all of the juicy details.

This is the story she told:

In January of 1988, Brando hired a new housekeeper for his Hollywood Hills home named Cristina Ruiz. At age twenty-nine, she was a smallish, dark-eyed woman with long black hair, a quick smile, and an abnormally large chest. A native Salvadorian, she had come to the States a year earlier to find work and a better life for herself. As a domestic, she was a quick learner and, after tutelage from the two other maids,

Thanks, PG!

she knew exactly how Marlon expected his house to be cleaned and run.

Some two months after she had proven herself a capable domestic, Brando started making sexual advances. She was twenty-nine and he was sixty-three. At first, she was afraid of him, but after assurances that he meant no harm, she gave in to his advances while continuing to live and work as a domestic at the Brando household. By May of 1989, she was pregnant, and visitors to the Hollywood Hills home as well as his children were witnesses to his dalliance.

When one of Brando's showbiz friends visited his Mulholland home and saw the pregnant maid, he asked Brando what had happened.

"It's nothing to worry about," he replied. "I'm going to do the right thing."

Several days later, although there was no legal ceremony, Brando gave her an engagement ring and a wedding ring. Also, he promised that, if she would remain loyal to him and care for his children, he would provide financial security for her and their children for the rest of her life.

When she was due, Brando went with her to the hospital in Santa Monica and watched the baby being born. Once the mother and child returned home, Brando made plans for Cristina's future and sent his minions to buy a home in San Fernando Valley for her and the child. Brando's massive Mulholland home was already inhabited by a throng of his children from other various wives and lovers as well as adopted children.

"At the moment," Melody concluded, "she still works at the Mulholland home during the day. At night, she stays at the home in the Valley. Marlon hired a driver to take her back and forth."

Thank God I had Melody. She had provided more than enough information to get my investigation started. Two days later, I drove over to the newly purchased home in the Valley to check things out. Located in North Hollywood, it was a modest affair by Tinseltown standards. I parked outside and waited. Around mid-morning, I watched curiously as an old white Cherokee pulled into the driveway and Brando, dressed in a house painter's hat and workman's clothes, his huge belly hanging over the belt, got out and went inside. After an hour, he emerged from the house and pulled a small lawn mower from the Cherokee and started mowing the grass. Once that was finished, he unfolded a small ladder and inspected the roof, then he took hedge trimmers and cut back some small bushes near the front door. Finally, exhausted from his labors, he went back inside.

Later that afternoon, I watched as Cristina served lunch on a small patio at the rear of the house. The new baby, sitting in a bassinet, was placed between them. As I watched Brando playing with his child and eating food prepared by the child's mother, I sensed that he was no longer a world famous movie star, but part of a regular, normal family.

As Brando had lunch with his maid and their love child, I pulled out my 35mm camera with the telephoto lens and started snapping photos. There were photos of Brando lovingly holding the child while Cristina fed it. There were photos of Brando kissing the sleeping child while Cristina held it in her lap. I was ecstatic at my luck. All were intimate, up close shots. Exactly what I wanted. I knew PG would be pleased.

On Thursday of the following week, the new edition hit the stands. The headlines blared: "Exclusive photos!! Brando and Maid with Love Child!! Intimate photos in their love nest!!"

After that scoop, I became the *Insider's* resident expert on Brando and Cristina. In the future, any time a new lead came across PG's desk about them, the assignment went to me.

Thanks, PG!

In early 1992, Cristina delivered a second child, a son. Brando was in New York on business and didn't attend the second birth, but he did make arrangements with his minions to see that Cristina had all of the comforts she required during his absence. Once he returned to LA, he realized he had a growing family with his housekeeper and felt it was time for a larger, more luxurious home.

In June of 1992, he shelled out $810,000 for a five-bedroom, three-bath home in Sherman Oaks. Unlike the first, it had all the trappings of Hollywood luxury. At over three thousand square feet, the home had a huge detached guesthouse, a family gazebo, sauna, pool, and a tennis court. After the purchase, Cristina asked that the small fence around the property be raised to over six feet high. She had heard the old Salvadorian myth that some Americans wanted to steal the eyes of small children and she wanted the fence high enough that outsiders couldn't see inside the property.

Several weeks later, Brando fulfilled her wishes and the fence was raised to almost seven feet high. I could no longer see inside the premises, but for more than a month, I watched as Brando and the old Cherokee went in and out of the security gate loaded with lumber, bricks, and other building materials. He was building a diving house at the pool for Christina and the kids. By then, Cristina had obtained a California driver's license and was the owner of a shiny new Mercedes.

In 1994, a third child, a boy, was born. After the birth of this child, Brando would spend ten to twelve days at a time with Cristina and their children. Frequently, on weekends, the couple and their children would be seen at amusement parks in Santa Monica and were frequently photographed in Beverly Hills shopping for clothes, books, and toys. Over the next few years, spending time with Christina and watching their children grow up became a mainstay in his life. The great movie star had finally become a staid old family man. He was seventy.

In late 2001, part of the support money which Brando had been providing Cristina stopped coming and she sued him for $100 million. She was still receiving the monthly money for child support, but money for the maintenance of the lavish Sherman Oaks home stopped. In the lawsuit, she noted that, although a portion of her support had stopped, both she and Brando continued to have a "cordial relationship for the children."

The money didn't stop because Brando had deserted her and the children or because he thought they didn't deserve it. It stopped because his health was failing. He'd been diagnosed with lung disease and huge medical bills had left him financially strapped. Due to his failing health, he was receiving little work, and the luxurious living he had become accustomed to finally caught up with him. The disease made breathing difficult and, wherever he went, he had to have a portable oxygen tank.

Brando died in July 2004 at UCLA Medical Center. His body was cremated and his ashes, along with those of two long-time friends, were scattered in Tahiti and Death Valley. His estate settled Cristina's lawsuit shortly after his death. Also, the luxurious home in Sherman Oaks, which had been in Brando's name, was transferred to her. With that, Brando had fulfilled the promise of financial security for Cristina and the children he had made fourteen years earlier.

Two weeks after Brando died, I had lunch with Melody in Westwood.

"It's so ironic," she said. "He had been married to some of the most beautiful women in the world, but Cristina was the only woman he ever truly loved. All of the other women in his life—actresses, dancers, models, singers, and personal assistants—all had some connection to show business."

Thanks, PG!

"So why would he want Cristina so much?" I asked.

"He knew she had no interest in using him," Melody said. "She was an uneducated Central American woman who loved him and wanted to please him only because he was Brando. She had no Hollywood ambitions. She loved Brando the man, not the big Hollywood star and Marlon knew it. He could be himself with her and didn't have to play the role of Hollywood star."

My conversation with Melody was a worthwhile lesson on Tinsel town. Hollywood stardom can be a beautiful dream come true, but it can also be an unimaginable curse that robs a person of their sense of what is truly valuable in the world.

Francesca

Hollywood is a cruel town, and it's obsessed with youth, beauty, and money in that order and nothing more. Every year, millions of men, women, and children from all over the world flock to Tinseltown with stars in their eyes. Unfortunately, many are called, but few are chosen. The winners live like royalty. The losers have to accept that fate and deal with the sadness of their unrealized dreams. This special cruelty takes a much larger, sadder toll on women than men. In most cases, as a woman's beauty fades, so does her career.

I first met Francesca in the summer of 1984. She was living in Studio City, just off Ventura Boulevard, in a two-bedroom apartment with her daughter Laura. Born in LA, she had childhood dreams of being a big star and when she graduated from Fairfax High School in 1956, the tall, statuesque Italian-American beauty could turn the heads of showbiz bigwigs, which won her small parts in movies and television.

In the late fifties, she was a regular on *The Fugitive*, and, after her husband died in 1960, she dated the show's handsome star for almost two years. In the early sixties, her beauty still intact, she found work playing nurses and appeared on several daytime game shows. By the late seventies, Francesca was in her late forties and, as her beauty started to fade, so did the parts. She still dated some of the big stars, but they tended to be older and their careers were on the wane.

By the early eighties, as her fortunes continued to diminish, she started to drink. Not a lot, but enough to soften the pain of the wrinkles and gray hair and to help her forget the cruelty of time and Hollywood. By the summer 1984, she was getting no work and, to make ends meet, she became a talent agent and a source for the *Insider*.

One of the television shows she worked on in the late sixties was a western titled *Cattle Drive,* which was about the daily lives and adventures of cattle herders. One of the show's stars was a man named Bronson Robert Cody, an Oklahoma native who had been a rodeo star before he started acting. Since he was billed as "Bronco Bob" during his rodeo days, he carried the same name over into his acting career. Tall, handsome, and well spoken, "Bronco Bob" had a special way with the ladies, and this didn't go unnoticed on the set.

During her work on the show, Francesca became friends with Roxy Wilson, a diminutive, dark-haired woman in her late twenties who was the show's script girl. Francesca knew that Roxanne had been dating "Bronco Bob," but she thought nothing of it until the day Roxy told her she was pregnant.

"I need your help," she told Francesca. "I'm three months pregnant with Bronco Bob's child and he wants to keep it a secret."

"How can I help?" Francesca asked.

"He wants to send me money to support the child, but not directly."

She explained that the show's star wanted to send support money to one of Roxy's friends or a family member rather

Thanks, PG!

than sending it directly to her. That way, the support money could never be traced back to him.

Francesca told her friend she would be happy to help.

Over the next eight years, Francesca would receive thousands of dollars in cash in the mail. There would be hundred-dollar bills stuffed in greeting cards. She would receive books with thousands of dollars slipped between the pages. Sometimes, rather than cash, there would be gift certificates for clothing and school supplies.

Francesca said the father never visited the child and, while the child knew that a famous star was her father, she never complained. When the child turned thirteen, the money stopped, Francesca said, and the mother and child moved to Colorado to be near her parents.

Meanwhile, Bronco Bob, who went on to become a Hollywood legend as an actor/producer/director, didn't acknowledge he was father of the child until 2002. By then, he had eleven children with nine different women.

In the fall of 1991, Francesca died of a massive stroke at age fifty-three. Not only had she been a bountiful and reliable source, but she'd been a gracious personal friend as well. A week after the funeral, I went to her apartment to pay my last respects. When I arrived, Laura was cleaning out her mother's room, which was stacked high with old photos, albums, letters, and movie memorabilia.

As she flipped through a stack of old pictures, my eyes suddenly fell on a photo of a beautiful Italian woman standing beside a man dressed in a Nineteenth Century English gentleman's costume. Immediately, I knew it was a scene from the movie *Five Weeks in a Balloon*, the movie that I had seen as a pharmacy student at Auburn University. I was thunderstruck. The beautiful Italian woman I had lusted after was Francesca and, for more than nine years, I hadn't known.

Like some miracle, PG had led me to her. I asked Laura if I could have the photo. She graciously handed it over and, to this day, it remains one of my happiest memories of Hollywood.

Sammy Davis Jr.

In the course of my career as a Hollywood reporter, I spent countless days and weeks on death watch stories, when the US and world press—depending on the degree of fame of the subject—would congregate outside the home or the hospital where the star was lying on his/her deathbed. But nothing had prepared me for what we witnessed at the time that beloved Sammy Davis Jr. was dying inside his Beverly Hills home.

Born in Harlem in 1925, Davis began his career in vaudeville at the age of three as a member of The Will Mastin Trio, a dancing and singing troupe that consisted of Davis, his father, and the group's namesake. After military service, Davis rejoined the group and they toured nationally, playing clubs, parties, and social events. Quickly, he began to achieve success on his own and became a recording artist and actor. He sang the title track for the 1954 film *Six Bridges to Cross* and later starred in the Broadway play *Mr. Wonderful*. In 1972, his song "The Candy Man Can" was the No. 1 single on the pop charts.

After becoming a member of the famous Frank Sinatra Rat Pack in 1959, he made several films with the group, and later had his own popular television show and became a headliner in Las Vegas.

At age twenty-nine, he lost his left eye in an auto accident, but the tragedy failed to dampen his love of show business. For almost a year, he wore a patch until he was fitted with a glass eye. Shortly afterward, he converted to Judaism.

Thanks, PG!

Ironically, the accident took him from being a well-known entertainer to a national celebrity.

He was a genius at making jokes about it.

Once before a golf match, Jack Benny asked Davis what his handicap was.

"Handicap?" Davis said. "Talk about handicap; I'm a one-eyed Negro Jew."

Over the years, that would become a signature quote for Davis.

In late 1989, Davis was diagnosed with throat cancer and doctors explained that surgery to remove his larynx would be the best solution. Davis replied he would rather keep his voice than have part of his throat removed and opted for a combination of radiation and chemotherapy. Although this helped for a while, his condition worsened only weeks afterward and doctors sadly announced they could do nothing more. Finally, over the days of May 13-16, 1990, the world's press converged on his home to await his death.

Never had I seen a mob of reporters like the one in front of Davis' Summit Drive home in Beverly Hills. A throng of more than three hundred journalists from around the world jammed traffic along the winding street and cops had to be called so the other residents of the exclusive canyon neighborhood could get in and out of their palatial homes.

Davis' next-door neighbor called police after reporters trampled his strawberry patch; his neighbor across the street turned on sprinklers daily to prevent reporters from sitting on the front lawn. Since there was no parking or sidewalks on Summit Drive, old friends, seeking to pay last respects, had to be dropped off. One showbiz friend in a wheelchair had to be wheeled almost two blocks to the house. Meanwhile, hungry reporters were taking photos and tag numbers of everyone who went in or came out of the house.

While the scene outside the home was nothing short of a three-ring circus, the scene inside was even more bizarre. Since late 1978, Davis had been a target of the IRS. The agency claimed that not only had he been under-reporting his taxes, but they had disallowed several shelters he had claimed in recent returns. Also, in recent years, the IRS had been confiscating all of his income from shows, tours, and Las Vegas appearances to pay off the debt. Now, as he lay dying, the tab was at $5.2 million and tax agents were not only assessing all of his personal possessions to sell at auction, but he was flat broke.

My source, a close friend of Davis's wife Altovise, said the home was a veritable treasure trove of showbiz memorabilia. There was an estimated $1.5 million in jewelry, an Andy Warhol soup can painting valued at $25,000, signed photos of Davis pals Elvis Presley and Marilyn Monroe, his lavish costumes, more than three hundred musical scores he had written, expensive Remington statuary, an eight-foot-high fiber glass statue of a character from the *Planet of the Apes* and awards, plaques, and gold watches he had accumulated over the years.

Since Davis was broke and all his assets frozen, his Rat Pack pal Frank Sinatra was paying the bills at the home for food, water, gas, and lights. While Davis' wife Altovise was also responsible for the debt, she publicly claimed she was penniless for fear the agents would seize any monies she might have. As a result, inside sources said the wife prayed every day that the utilities in the home would remain in service until her husband died.

Finally, around noon on May 16, the publicist and the family announced Davis had passed. All of the busy hustle-bustle, the throng of world press, the cops, and the distraught neighbors were gone now. All that was remained were memories.

Thanks, PG!

I think you could make the argument that, upon a celebrity's death, the reach of his fame can be determined by the geographical representation of the reporters assigned to cover his demise. I had covered my share of deathwatches, but I had never seen as broad a representation of world press as the one for Sammy Davis Jr.

When I covered the wedding of Robert Wagner and Jill St. John in the Palisades, there was a reporter from Turkey. That was the first time I had ever seen a press rep from such a far-flung locale.

At Sammy Davis Jr.'s death watch, there was not only a reporter from Turkey, but press reps from England, France, Japan, and even Vietnam, probably the result of Davis' appearances as an entertainer for our servicemen during the Vietnam War. It was the one and only time I had ever seen a reporter from Vietnam at any Hollywood event. It was a first and a moment to be remembered. Now that's what I call true worldwide fame.

Fran Levington

No single story I ever wrote for the *Insider* touched my heart in quite the same way as a deathbed interview with Fran Levington, the puppeteer genius who won the hearts and minds of millions of television viewers in the mid-to-late fifties as "Fran" in the beloved children's television show *Kukla, Fran and, Ollie*.

While chatting with one of my medical sources about a big star who had recently had surgery, the person said, "Do you know who Fran Levington is? She was on *Kukla, Fran, and Ollie* during the early days of television. And she's dying of bone marrow cancer."

I was still drawing a blank. Finally, we ended the call and I went to lunch. An hour later, sitting over a Chinese chicken salad at Chin-Chin's on Sunset Blvd., it dawned on me. *Kukla, Fran, and Ollie* was an early television puppet show that featured Fran, the only human on the show, Kukla, the bulb-nosed, bald-headed, head honcho of a puppet troupe and Ollie, a mischievous, one-tooth dragon.

The puppets said their lines on a make-believe children's stage while Fran, who played big sister to the troupe and tried to maintain peace among them, was outside the stage. It was a marvelously simple, but highly effective entertainment vehicle.

Instantly, my mind wandered back to the late fifties when I was a student in junior high and, every day after school, I would rush into the house, throw my books on the couch, and flip on the television to watch the *KFO* show on an old black and white TV that received only two channels.

I was twelve or thirteen years old, but I remember how I would giggle with delight when Ollie would slam his flat chin on the stage in frustration or do a rolling motion on his back to endear himself to Fran and the audience. Although the show was developed for children, often the themes were very adult. With that sudden flash of memory, I knew I had to interview her.

That afternoon, I went to the hospital in Van Nuys. When I entered the room, I explained who I was. She graciously shook my hand and asked me to sit down.

She was dressed in a light-blue hospital gown and her snowy white hair hung loosely about her shoulders. Although I could see she was very sick, she had a quick smile, a mischievous twinkle in her eyes, and was eager to talk to me.

She was eighty-one years old.

"Oh, I love the *Insider*," she said when I announced my affiliation. "They have great recipes and housekeeping tips and I love to read the latest Hollywood gossip. How much time will you need?"

"Probably thirty minutes to an hour."

Thanks, PG!

"Then we better wait until tomorrow," she said. "In a few minutes, I'm going in for radiation treatment and I'll be very tired after that, but tomorrow morning, say around ten, I'd love to do the interview."

I smiled and said thanks.

"Be sure you're here tomorrow morning," she said. "I might not be here tomorrow afternoon."

"Ten sharp," I replied.

The following morning when I arrived at her room, she welcomed me.

Although she put on a cheerful face, I could see she was near death. Her hair, which had been snowy white the day before, was now a parched brown color and hung scraggily and lifeless about her shoulders. Somehow, the radiation had affected her eyes and she kept moving her head to and fro as if she were trying to keep me in focus.

"Let's get started. I'm going to meet Archie," she said, referring to her late husband, "and we've got a long journey ahead of us."

She recalled her early days in Iowa and how she was born for show business.

"When I was a teenager in Iowa, my brother put together a local orchestra and hired me as a singer. From the very first show, I was hooked."

Later, she worked in Cedar Rapids, then moved to Chicago, where she found work as a singer and comedienne and was an instant hit as "Aunt Franny," a gossipy spinster on Chicago radio.

"Although I could sing and act," she said, "it was comedy and puppets that I loved most."

In 1947, while living in Chicago, she met an old puppeteer friend she had known from her War Bonds tour days and he asked her to put together a children's show with puppets.

"I had had the idea in my head for *Kukla, Fran, and Ollie* for almost thirty years," she said. "It was very similar to a puppet show I did at my school when I was a teenager. I just renamed the characters and wrote new skits."

It was an instant hit.

"I'll always be remembered for *Kukla, Fran, and Ollie,*" she said. "I loved doing that show. You can discuss very serious subjects in an innocent way with puppets and not offend or upset anyone."

She said her maiden name was Allison, but she later married a music publisher named Archie Levington who had died in 1978.

"We never had any children," she said. "My children were the millions of kids who watched *Kukla, Fran, and Ollie* day after day."

I smiled.

"And I loved every one of them," she said.

I explained that I had been one of her adoring fans.

"Then you're one of my children, Billy Don," she said, "and I love you."

Suddenly, my mind was flooded with all the wonderful memories of the afternoons I had spent watching *KFO*. The willful, overbearing Kukla, the well meaning, but simple Ollie, and the reasoning voice and the counsel of Fran came roaring back into my mind as if I were suddenly transported back to 1957.

"I love you too," I said, and from the bottom of my heart, I meant it.

She smiled.

"I think I'll sleep now," she said.

"I understand," I replied. "Thanks for the interview."

For a moment, I peered at her as she closed her eyes and drifted off to sleep.

Thanks, PG!

The following morning, I called the hospital. The operator said she had died at eleven a.m. the previous day. She never awoke from sleep after my interview.

As I hung up the phone, tears were streaming down my face and I wasn't sure why. I had only known this woman through her television show and our two brief encounters at the Van Nuys hospital, yet somehow, I felt I had been friends with her all my life.

To me, there was always a special sadness in seeing an entertainer die. Here was a kind, gracious, loving woman who brought joy to millions and now, like many human beings, her ultimate reward was to die alone. Probably, more than anything, I was made aware of my own mortality. In my heart, I knew that each of us must face death in our own way. I had watched this wonderful person walk that lonesome valley. Many times, I've wondered how I would face my own death.

John Isaac Jones

Chapter 13
Hollywood Stories II

Daniel

Long before the advent of television, Harry Morgan had made a big name for himself in films after appearing in a string of westerns and black and white dramas playing judges, sheriffs, preachers, and country doctors. When television came along, he played sidekick to Sgt. Joe Friday in the popular series *Dragnet*. Later, he would win international recognition as "The Colonel" in the long-running television hit *M*A*S*H*, a series about a medical surgical unit in the Korean War.

In the late summer of 1989, Harry, at age seventy-two, was shooting a made-for-TV film in Arizona when he received a mysterious phone call. Upon finishing the call, he went straight to the director and told him he had a "family emergency" in LA and was leaving the set. When the director reminded him they were in the middle of a production, Harry shouted, "Screw the production. I'm going back to LA."

"I'll sue," the director protested.

"Sue all you want," Harry said. "This is something I have to do."

When he arrived at LAX, Harry went straight to his home in Pacific Palisades, packed four days' change of clothes, then set off for West Hollywood. He was due to meet a physician's

Thanks, PG!

assistant from the local hospital at two p.m. The physician's assistant had made the mysterious call.

The father of three boys, Morgan had known for some time that his youngest son was gay. Harry had many gay friends in Hollywood; he'd learned to accept them and work with them and made it a point to never judge anyone by their sexual preferences. At family functions, while his other sons appeared with wives and girlfriends, Daniel always attended with Greg, his longtime friend and "partner." Harry's long-time wife Barbara, who had passed several years earlier, never mentioned the subject.

Twenty minutes later, Harry pulled up in front of his son's apartment building and went to the door. The PA opened the door and greeted him. The PA, a short, heavy-set Latino man named Leo, explained that he worked for the local AIDS project. They shook hands and went directly to Daniel's room. For a long moment, Harry peered down at his sleeping, severely emaciated son.

"Your son has the most virulent strain of HIV known to modern medicine," the PA began. "This strain destroys the neuromuscular system and normal functions such as muscle control, limb movement, and chewing deteriorates rapidly."

Morgan didn't reply.

"You realize your own life is in danger," Leo continued. "You'll have to wear a mask and gloves at all times and be very careful to not come in contact with his body fluids."

"I can handle it," the actor interrupted again, raising his voice. "He is my son."

The PA explained that a male nurse from the local AIDS support group would come every day to change bed linens, update the drip, and sterilize his son's eating utensils. He told Harry the spare bedroom was safe for habitation.

"He can't chew, so all of his food will have to be softened into liquid and spoon-fed to him," the PA continued. "It's mostly baby food, like mashed peas, bananas, peaches, and such."

"What can I expect?"

"There's significant loss of mental and motor skills," Leo continued. "There's some-" He stopped before he said the word "dementia."

"His mind comes and goes?" Morgan asked.

Leo nodded.

"What about medications?"

"All that can help him is the morphine drip for pain."

Harry cleared his throat before asking the big question.

"How long does he have?"

"A few days. A week at most."

A long silence.

"Leave me with him," Harry said finally.

"Remember all the precautions," the PA said. "You can call me if you have questions."

After the PA left, Morgan hauled his clothes and shaving gear from the car. Once he was settled, he went to the kitchen, retrieved a pair of rubber gloves and a facemask, and read the feeding instructions. Finally, he took a seat at his son's bedside and started to read.

Some twenty minutes later, Daniel woke up.

"Dad," the son said. "I'm so glad to see you."

"I came to be with you for a while," Morgan said.

"Thanks," the son replied. "Why isn't Mom here?"

Harry didn't know how to answer at first.

"Oh, she's been very busy lately," he said. "You know, she's got work to do at home."

"Will she come visit me too?"

"Maybe she'll be along later. When do you want to eat?" the father asked.

"Never," the son replied. "I can't taste anything."

"You've got to eat something."

Thanks, PG!

The son laughed weakly.

Harry didn't reply.

Neither could utter the stark reality of the situation.

"Daddy, why did you come to be with me at a time like this?"

"When the older boys were younger," Morgan said finally, "I had lots of free time in my career. When you came along, suddenly, every time I finished one movie, another one was waiting."

For several minutes, neither of them spoke. Each was trying to digest the previous conversation.

"I'm glad you're here now," Daniel said finally.

"I'm glad I'm here too," the actor replied.

After talking for almost an hour, the son fell asleep. Harry went into the kitchen and blended a small bowl of bananas and peaches, then placed it in the refrigerator. Next, he checked on his son, who was still resting, then left the apartment and walked to a small restaurant nearby. He had spaghetti and meatballs with Texas Toast. When he arrived back at the apartment, his son was still sleeping.

The following morning, Morgan was up at seven. When he went into Daniel's room, his son was staring out the window.

"Good morning, son," Harry said, dangling a packet of old photos.

Once seated, he opened the packet and started thumbing through them.

"Remember this one?" Harry said, holding a photo in front of his son. "Me and you and Mom and your brothers visiting the San Diego Zoo."

Daniel peered at the photo.

"I remember the big snake," Daniel said.

"It was a twenty-three-foot reticulated python, and they fed it live chickens."

"Yeah!" Daniel replied excitedly, his eyes lighting up with recognition. "I felt so sorry for those poor chickens. I've always been afraid of snakes."

Over the next two hours, father and son remembered the good times. Around three p.m., Daniel said he was tired and wanted to sleep.

After the son drifted off to sleep, Harry went for a walk at a small park near the apartment and, after watching a group of children playing soccer for almost an hour, he returned to the apartment. Daniel was still asleep. Morgan watched television until just past nine p.m., then went to bed.

Around two a.m., he was awakened by the sound of his son's voice.

"Daddy! Daddy!" the muted voice called.

Instantly, Morgan was out of bed and at his son's bedside.

When he flipped on the light, he could see the genuine terror in his son's eyes.

"What's wrong, son?"

"The snake! The big snake!" the son said. "I can see him. I can see him, Daddy!"

"Son," Harry said consolingly, "it was only a dream."

Daniel looked into his father's eyes. He was calmer now.

"Go back to sleep," the father said. "Everything is going to be fine."

"I'm afraid, Daddy," the son said fearfully. "I'm so afraid."

"It's going to be okay," the father said, comforting his son. "Everything is going to be all right."

For some ten minutes, Harry sat quietly at his son's bedside. Finally, when he was certain his son was asleep again, he returned to the other bedroom.

The following morning, Morgan was awake at seven. When he appeared at his son's bedside, Daniel had raised himself to one elbow. He was staring at the ceiling and making a waving motion with his free hand. For several

Thanks, PG!

moments, the son didn't realize his father was in the room, then suddenly, Daniel glanced at him.

"Dad! Dad!" he said excitedly. "Look at my kite. See how high it is."

Harry looked up at the ceiling.

"Yeah, it's way up there," he replied.

"If I had more string, it would go higher," Daniel said. "Can you get me some more string?"

"Sure, sure," Morgan said. "We'll ask Mom to buy more string."

For several moments more, Daniel continued gazing at the ceiling, then finally slumped back into the bed and was fast asleep.

At 10:30, Harry, for no particular reason, blended two more jars of bananas, peaches, and milk and took the bowl to his son's bedside. After some twenty minutes, the son awoke, then Morgan raised his son to a slightly upright position and offered him a spoonful of food.

"Take a bite," Morgan said.

The son took a taste and grimaced.

"Oh, I can't do that," he said.

Morgan looked at his son, then returned to the kitchen and placed the blend in the refrigerator. Around 2:30 p.m., Daniel awoke. Harry glanced up from his reading. His son had raised himself on one elbow and was peering out the window.

"Dad! Dad!" he said anxiously.

"Son! I'm here," Morgan replied, taking his son's hand in his own. "I'm here."

"Look! Look!" the son said, peering out the window.

"What is it?" the father asked.

"It's the snake!" the son said, his eyes widening in genuine fear. "I can see him! I can see him!"

"It's okay, son," the father said, standing over him and still holding his son's hand. "He won't hurt you. Be brave."

"Daddy, I'm so cold," he said. "I'm so cold."

Morgan could see that his son was trembling.

Then he watched as Daniel slumped back on the bed.

For several moments, he stood over his son. Suddenly, the son began taking deeper and deeper breaths and then, as Harry watched, the breathing became more and more labored until the sounds of his son's breathing reverberated throughout the room, and finally, the entire apartment. Just as suddenly as the labored breathing began, it stopped. Harry placed his hand on his son's chest. There was no heartbeat. He touched his son's forehead. It was growing cold. For several minutes, he held his hand on Daniel's forehead until the warmth was gone, then he went to the living room and picked up the phone.

"Leo?" he said.

There was a pause.

"I think my son is dead," Harry said.

When the PA arrived, he went straight to the son's bed and placed a stethoscope on his chest.

"He's gone."

For a minute, the famous actor sat motionless in the chair, then, overcome with emotion, he went to the nearby bedroom and began sobbing. As the PA unhooked the morphine drip, placed the son's arms over his chest, then covered the body with a clean sheet, Harry Morgan, his head in his hands, wept like a child.

After Morgan's publicist denied that Daniel had died of AIDS, the company lawyers said I would need an official cause of death before publication, so I flew to Sacramento to get the death certificate. In the years that followed, Morgan never talked about the incident. The subject was not mentioned in his memoirs, in conversations with friends, or reported in the mainstream press. After Morgan died in 2011, the only mention of his son in the obituary was that Daniel "had succumbed" at age twenty-nine. As always, Hollywood swept the subject of homosexuality and its trappings under the rug.

Outside of the story that appeared in the *Insider*, no one else knew about this incident except Morgan, his son, me, and my source Leo, the male nurse. The *Insider* paid Leo ten thousand dollars plus expenses to install a recording device with a voice-activated microphone in the closet of Daniel's room. Once Daniel's body was removed, Leo presented me with three cardboard boxes full of recorded tapes. This story was written from those tapes. It took me five days to transcribe over 150 hours of recordings.

Raymond Burr

Homosexuality had been an integral part of Hollywood culture since the inception of the motion picture industry. From Hollywood's earliest days, thousands upon thousands of gay men had proven themselves in behind-the-camera posts such as casting, wardrobe, makeup, cameramen, and even as directors and producers. When a gay man became a major box office star, the studio bosses expected and even demanded that the star's sexual orientation be kept a closely guarded secret. After all, Hollywood's leading men were expected to portray the type of virile male that made women swoon and men cheer. Any hint that the actor was not a macho man hunk was absolutely not tolerated in public.

Actor Raymond Burr, the subject of this story, learned early on as his star rose in Hollywood, that his sexual orientation could wreck his career. His life was a sad and ongoing battle to hide his homosexuality.

A native of Canada, little was known about Burr's childhood. His father ran a hardware store and his mother was a music teacher in British Columbia, but beyond that, few hard facts were available. Although there were numerous stories about trips to China with his parents and tales of various marriages and children, the only fact that could be proven about Burr was that, as a small boy, he would spend endless hours in the family garden growing and cultivating roses.

As an adult, Burr was a burly, gravel-voiced bear of a man who broke into Hollywood as a heavy during the film noir craze of the fifties. Breaking bones and making violent threats was his stock in trade during those years and he appeared in more than forty, mostly gangster, films with some of the biggest stars of the day. In 1960, he was cast in the title role of Perry Mason, the most famous defense attorney in television history that always won his case with a daring last-minute on-the-stand revelation or confession.

The same year he got the contract, Raymond met Robert Benavides, an aspiring young actor and Korean War veteran who had a job on the series. They quickly became lovers and, shortly afterward, Raymond got Robert a permanent, behind-the-camera spot on the show that eventually led to him becoming a producer. Although they would be "partners" for more than thirty years, they both knew they had to keep their relationship a closely guarded secret.

Over the ensuing years, a conspiracy of lies and fabrications involving publicists, show regulars, gossip columnists, and even Raymond himself managed to keep his secret hidden. Publicists regularly planted stories that he was dating various young starlets and, during the late fifties, even arranged dates between Burr and several beautiful aspiring actresses so directors and producers could see them on the arm of a big star. Although a sham, it was a win-win for all parties.

In truth, Burr was briefly married to an actress during his early days in Tinseltown. Although the union was brief, this information was played up front and center in all of his professional bios and press releases. Hedda Hopper, the most famous gossip columnist of the day, never divulged his secret

Thanks, PG!

because her son William played Perry Mason's sidekick private investigator on the show. When regulars on the show were asked about Burr's homosexuality, they always dodged the subject with the comment, "It's none of my business."

Over the years, Raymond and Robert built a vast business empire that included exotic orchids, fine wine, seashells, Portuguese water dogs, and extensive real estate holdings, which included homes in LA, Hawaii, and an island in the South Seas. These business interests enabled them to live the life of royalty. In 1974, they bought an old farm in Sonoma's Dry Creek Valley and developed it as a winery that was named after Burr upon his death and still bears his name.

While Burr was active to some degree in all of their businesses, his favorite was the orchid business where he cultivated and crossbred exotic orchids. His holdings included nurseries in California, Hawaii, the Azores, and the South Seas. His favorites were exotic black orchids, and Burr would spend endless days in his California nursery, making copious notes and studying the characteristics of various sub-species. Over the course of his work, he added more than 1300 new species to the worldwide catalogue.

"The genome of the rose is child's play when compared to the complexity of the orchid genome," he once said. "Studying the intricacies of the orchid genome is like listening to a Beethoven symphony."

In late 1992, Burr was diagnosed with kidney cancer and doctors urged that the cancerous kidney be removed. Only days after the surgery, he began experiencing excruciating pain and, after further examination, doctors reported the cancer had spread into the lungs and liver and was now inoperable. At the news, Burr said he wanted to return to the Sonoma ranch to spend his last days.

Only days after this story broke, Simon called me.

"Perry Mason is dying," he said. "We have a source in Santa Rosa who is friends with the nurse in attendance. All you got to do is go there and wait until he dies. Don't hesitate to push her for details. We're paying her lots of money for the exclusive story."

The following day, I was on a plane to Healdsburg, California to meet the source. At the meeting, we agreed she would call me twice a day over the following week with updates on Burr's condition. If he died, she was to call me immediately. On Friday afternoon, she called and reported Burr was dead. I asked about his final hours.

This is the story she told.

On the morning of September 3, 1993, Burr, who had been on a morphine drip for over two weeks, awoke, turned to Robert, and asked about the status of the ranch's chardonnay grapes, the livestock, and his beloved orchids.

Robert knew the end was near, and his eyes filled with tears as his long-time partner asked questions about ranch operations as if he were going to be there forever.

"What about the Bulbophyllum Filiforme specimens in nursery number four?" Burr asked. "We had thirty-two new specimens in early August. Are they healthy and blooming?"

"They're fine," Robert replied.

A long silence.

"Ray," Robert said tenderly, taking his hand, "I wanted to thank you for the wonderful life we've had together. I couldn't have asked for a more wonderful friend and partner."

"You realize," Burr said, "the Filiforme has to have a constant temperature of at least 64 degrees or they'll wither and die. As natives of West Africa, their genome requires much warmer temperatures than other orchids."

"Yes, Ray," Robert replied. "I know, but this is not really the time to be discussing business. We should—"

Thanks, PG!

"I can't wait until the black Filiforme are adult plants," Burr continued. "The differentiation between the jet black colors and the green is absolutely amazing. Once we have adults, I want several brought into the ranch house. Maybe one in the sitting room by the zebra and another on the Italian marble table beside the fireplace."

"Ray," Robert said again, trying to get his attention.

"No, on the mantel; that's where I want them," Burr continued. "I can see them now, those glossy black colors against the royal blue wallpaper."

"Ray," Robert said. "I'm trying to say goodbye."

"And what about the pink Orchondrinea?" Burr said. "Are the nursery workers aware of their sunlight requirements?"

Robert could see he was getting nowhere.

"You never listen to me," he said sadly.

"Now be sure you tell Carlos that the newer pink Bienchadea orchids in nursery number six require..."

Suddenly, the diatribe stopped. For a moment, Burr looked straight at Robert as if he were about to say something important, then he slowly slumped backward on his pillow. Around noon, he slipped into a coma and died.

The following week, when the story was printed, there was only a tiny blurb on the front page which read: "Raymond Burr's Final Hours!!" Inside, however, the story got a full-blown centerfold spread.

The headlines blared: "Perry Mason Makes Deathbed Request!! Long-time Lover Sadly Watches Famous Actor Die!!" There was even a photo of me with my byline.

His obituary, which appeared in newspapers and magazines throughout the world, represented little more than the fabrications, the lies, and half-truths which had been disseminated over the years by publicists and Burr himself. The conspiracy to hide the truth about Burr's homosexuality was complete.

Only after his death did books and magazine articles start to print the truth. Interestingly enough, at the time of his death, Hollywood had considerably softened its posture on homosexuality, probably because of the massive publicity generated by the AIDS epidemic. In the late eighties and early nineties, studios and big stars felt it was good public relations to support AIDS projects. While several big stars and studio executives were openly gay, the unspoken strictures that Burr had faced were somewhat loosened. Burr, with an intricately woven web of protective lies and half-truths, had borne the brunt of the discrimination and had weathered it quite well.

Thanks, PG!

Chapter 14
Hollywood Stories III

Stage Mother

Berniece Jannsen was the poster child for stage mothers all over the world. After spending more than forty years guiding her son to the furthermost heights of Hollywood stardom, she sadly watched as the fruits of that success—the money, the women and the drugs—destroyed her creation.

A natural beauty, Berniece burst into the national spotlight in 1928 as an eighteen-year-old beauty queen when she won the Miss Nebraska title in her native state. Four months later, she was named a finalist in the International Pageant of Pulchritude, the forerunner of the Miss Universe contest. While touring with the Miss Universe entourage, she caught the eye of Florenz Ziegfeld, the master showman behind the world-famous "Ziegfeld Follies," and he signed her on to be in such Broadway hits as *Rio Rita* and *The Girl from Toledo*.

After her contract expired, she returned to Nebraska and married a local banker, and, in March of 1931, she had a son, David, who would become her life.

"After two years of marriage, I knew I had no intention of spending my life in rural Nebraska as a banker's wife," Berniece said. "During the Ziegfeld days, I had been hooked on show business, and I had dreams of bigger and better things for me and my son."

In 1937, she filed for divorce, and once it was final, she took her beloved David and set off to Hollywood.

"It was a two-day train ride from Omaha to Los Angeles," Berniece recalled, "and the minute we arrived, we went straight to Swensen's Ice Cream on Hollywood Boulevard. As we sat eating our French Vanilla, I told David someday he was going to have a star on the sidewalk right out front."

After renting a small apartment in the Fairfax district, she set about making a star of her son.

"Day after day, we would go to casting calls and auditions at the major studios, community theaters, and little theater groups," she said. "In those days, the Pasadena Playhouse was the launch pad for new talent, so I worked extra hard to get David in there."

Sometimes, she said, she and her son would go to six or seven auditions in a week and come away empty-handed.

"Why didn't they like me?" she recalled David asking on the way home.

"I would explain that he did nothing wrong. The director simply felt that some other child was a better fit for the part. That kind of rejection is tough on a young child."

Despite the setbacks, Berniece kept plugging away and, finally, parts started coming in. There was a part in *Peter Pan*, a part in a famous Eugene O'Neill play, and, finally, a major role in an early production of *The King and I*.

"In late 1940, money got tight, work dropped off, and I had a bout of appendicitis," Berniece said. "I had no choice but to put David in a boys' home until I could get on my feet again."

From the very first, her son absolutely hated the boys' home in San Dimas.

"He felt so alone in there, and he hated the other boys, but it wasn't all that bad," she said. "The place was clean and the food was good, but they had strict rules. I think that's what

Thanks, PG!

David hated, having to follow the rules. He came home every Sunday, and it was only for eight months."

David got his big break in 1957 when he was signed for the title role in the television drama, *Richard Diamond, Private Detective*, a series about a suave private eye who cruised around LA in a convertible.

"The day he signed the contract was the happiest day of my life," Berniece said. "After the signing, David went straight out and bought a brand new 1956 Thunderbird and spent all day washing, cleaning, and shining it. This was the day we had been waiting for. David was on his way."

The following year, David married Ellie Graham, a model and interior decorator he'd met a year earlier at a studio wrap party.

"Next to me, his first wife was the best thing that ever happened to him," Berniece said. "She absolutely worshipped the ground he walked on, and she had a business sense that not even I had. I knew how to dress him up and coach him and get him in front of directors, but Ellen knew how to do deals."

In early 1963, when David was negotiating his contract for *The Fugitive* with studio bosses, Berniece said Ellie told him he should ask for thirty percent of the gross. When she said that, Berniece said David's jaw dropped.

"You're the heart and soul of the show," Berniece quoted Ellie saying. "Without you, they have nothing. You're worth every last penny of it."

David reluctantly followed her advice and, sure enough, he did get twenty-two percent of the gross which, according to Berniece, was unheard of at the time.

Over the next four years, *The Fugitive,* a continuing story about a physician on the lam after being wrongfully convicted of killing his wife, became one of the most popular series in the history of television and would make him a multi-millionaire.

Despite Ellie's business talents, the handsome star was incapable of remaining faithful. After the first few flings, he promised to change, but fidelity was not part of his nature. Over time, arguments over his infidelities led to violent domestic disputes and, finally, they divorced in 1970.

"Ellie said her life ended with the divorce," Berniece recalled. "She never remarried and ended up writing a book about their relationship. She finally died of a broken heart."

During the first marriage, the couple had accumulated wealth beyond their wildest dreams. They owned a vacation home on Maui, a glass penthouse in Century City, two Rolls-Royces, a yacht harbored at Marina Del Rey and a $1.5 million beach house in Malibu.

In 1975, David married a second time to a shapely model and Hollywood serial wife who had a reputation as "the hostess with the most-est." Fourteen months into the marriage, they separated, and David was seen publicly with a long list of starlets.

The second marriage was little more than a prolonged adventure into women and drugs. Although Berniece never admitted that David used cocaine—she always claimed it was alcohol—one Hollywood source said during the last few years of his life, he was spending up to two thousand dollars a week on cocaine.

"Sometimes, he would make three trips a week to his dealer's home in Carbon Canyon to buy 'snow,'" the source said. "He always had to have two lines in the morning, another after lunch, and still another before the evening meal. I knew his heart wouldn't last long."

The days at the orphanage had left deep emotional scars. At parties, after a few drinks, he would cry openly about his days in the orphanage," David's friend said. "'My mother put me in prison with the scum of the earth,' he would say. 'I had played to packed houses at Pasadena Playhouse and all these

Thanks, PG!

kids had to show for their lives were missing teeth and bitter memories.'" Other partygoers would slip away from David and tell their friends, "David's back in the boys' home again."

The last forty-eight hours of his life were nothing short of a Bacchanalian orgy. On the first day, there was a married woman in Santa Monica, then a threesome at the home of a producer in Bel-Air and, finally, a long romp with a teenage groupie in the Hollywood Hills. The second day, he was back with the married woman, then two hours of drinking and snorting at the Century City penthouse, and finally, a tryst with an old high school sweetheart at the Chateau Marmont. Late that night, he returned to his second wife at their Malibu home.

Early the following morning, the second wife was awakened by a choking sound.

"I thought he was choking on some of the butterscotch cookies I had made the night before," she said. "It never occurred to me that he was having a heart attack."

Berniece said almost an hour passed before an ambulance was called and, by then, it was too late.

"His death almost killed me," Berniece recalled. "For over a week, I couldn't get out of bed. The doctor said the depression had so weakened my immune system that I had a cancer in my neck and under my right arm. As I lay in the hospital recovering, it crossed my mind to just go ahead and die, but somehow, I knew I had to live to carry on David's name."

Over the following years, she accepted her son's star on Hollywood Boulevard, making sure it was placed in the exact spot in front of Swensen's where she and David had had French Vanilla ice cream some thirty years earlier. She launched a fan club, which ultimately would have over 20,000 members, and created a webpage documenting David's life and achievements.

The last time I saw Berniece was in the fall of 1994. She had been a source and personal friend for seven of the ten years I had worked in Hollywood. Often, on Sunday afternoons, she would invite me to her small condo in Tarzana for tea and cucumber sandwiches.

During that final visit, I could still see the fierce, strong-willed, independence that more than fifty years earlier had driven her to sweep up her young son from a small town in the Midwest and flee to Hollywood to make him a star. I asked what she had learned as a stage mother.

She smiled, but I could see the bitterness.

"The second wife succeeded in taking him away from me," she said. "She fed his nightmares about the orphanage and poisoned his mind about all the ways I had taken advantage of his talents. She not only took him away from me emotionally, but financially as well."

"What do you mean?" I asked.

"She convinced him to leave me out of his will."

"You got nothing for all the years you put into him?"

She shook her head sadly.

"He left me a dollar."

"Didn't you feel that was unfair?" I asked.

"Of course," she said. "Even worse than that, I never even got the dollar, but that's all right. He did what he had to do in this world and I did the same. I'll always love him. I'm his mother."

Berniece died at the Motion Picture Country Hospital in Woodland Hills in 1995. She was eighty-five.

Olivia

As a Hollywood reporter, you never knew how people were going to react when they learned you worked for the *Insider*. In some cases, they absolutely hated you because they

Thanks, PG!

knew you are out to reveal the most closely guarded secrets of their favorite stars. On the other hand, there remained a closeted group of gossip-lovers who felt their lives would be indescribably empty without a weekly dose of Hollywood scandal. These closeted gossip lovers tended to hide away in secret places and, although they loved reading the *Insider*, they would have been horrified if anyone discovered their secret passion. Discovering these people was always a wonderful surprise.

In the late spring of 1992, a famous Hollywood couple who had been the toast of the town for many years were divorced and the male portion of the famous duo found new love with Olivia, a young secretary who lived near UCLA. Once word of the affair surfaced, PG sent word to the LA bureau he wanted a full story and photos. Two sources quickly provided ample fodder for a full-blown story on Olivia, but there were no photos. The photo desk had scanned local newspaper archives and photo services, but no pictures of Olivia were to be found. Finally, a photographer and I were assigned to get photos.

For two full days, the photographer and I waited outside her West LA home. In the late afternoon of the second day, she pulled into the driveway and the photographer and I went to the door.

When she opened the door, we announced who we were. Olivia was elated, then stepped outside to see if any neighbors were about.

"Quick! Come inside!" she said.

Once we were inside, the photographer and I could see huge stacks of *Insider* editions on the coffee table.

"As you can see," she said, "I'm a huge fan of your publication."

Once we explained we wanted photos of her, she explained that she would rather give us several old photos of herself rather than make a new one.

"That way, I know exactly what is going to be printed."

We agreed and, moments later, she produced a shoebox filled with old photos. Finally, after some thirty minutes, she had selected several of her liking. One shot was made at Zuma Beach and depicted her in a sexy pose leaning against a "No Parking" sign. There was another steamy photo of her at Santa Monica pier and still another on a fishing trip in Northern California.

"I like this one," I said, indicating a shot of her with her parents.

"Oh, no," she replied. "It's not sexy enough."

Then she produced a topless photo.

"The boss would never approve that," I said. "We're a family magazine."

"You could black out the nipples," she suggested.

"No way PG would ever approve that," I said.

She shrugged. "Okay," she said. "Take these and use the ones you like."

We put the selected photos in an envelope and started to leave. Quickly, she was at the door and peeked outside for any neighbors.

"Hurry!" she said. "I can't be seen with you guys."

"Your neighbors don't know who we are," I said.

"I can't take any chances," she replied.

We started out.

"Wait!" she said.

I turned.

"See if you can get it on the front page," she whispered.

"I will," I whispered back.

Two weeks later, after the story appeared on the front page, I got a thank-you card in the mail with a hundred-dollar gift certificate. She said all of her friends loved it. Exhibitionism is alive and well and can be found in some of the most unexpected places.

Michaeo! Michaeo! We Love You!

During my years as a celebrity reporter, I thought I had seen celebrity worship in all of its possible incarnations until one day in the summer of 1993 in Mexico City. Earlier that year, Michael Jackson, the self-proclaimed King of Pop, and probably one of the true musical geniuses of the twentieth century, was accused of molesting a child by the Los Angeles prosecutor's office.

For many years, one of his closest friends had been the world-famous actress Elizabeth Taylor. The singer had actually created a shrine in his home for her and, in times of trouble, considered her his "personal advisor." Thus, after the molestation charges, the singer asked her to meet him at the Chapultepec Hotel in Mexico City for a week to "discuss the matter." For the occasion, they had rented the entire top story of the hotel.

Once local newspapers and television outlets announced that "Michaeo" was going to be staying in the hotel, thousands of Mexican girls, mostly teenagers, started milling around the hotel's front entrance hoping to catch a glimpse of their hero. After the fans proved to be a nuisance to hotel guests, hotel security cordoned off the front entrance and sidewalks leading to the entrance and relegated the fans to a grassy area in front of the hotel.

On the day I arrived, some 200 to 300 howling Mexican girls were packed onto the grassy area, lying on their backs and peering up at the hotel's top floor.

"Michaeo! Michaeo! We love you!" they screamed over and over at the top of their lungs.

Space on the grassy area came at a price. If one girl grew tired and gave up her spot, another girl quickly jumped in to occupy the space. Catfights, hair pulling, and scratching broke out between some of the girls as they fought ferociously to win a spot on the grass.

On Saturday afternoon, all hell broke loose when the famous singer appeared on the hotel balcony and waved to his adoring fans. At the sight of "Michaeo," the girls went berserk. At the height of the frenzy, "Michaeo" started dropping toy teddy bears from the balcony to the crowd below.

As teddy bears started to rain down on the crowd, the girls went into an absolute frenzy. One girl jumped up to catch a falling teddy bear. Once she had it in hand, another girl tried to snatch it away and the toy bear was ripped apart in the ensuing tugging match. These girls were fighting one another with bare fists to get one of the teddy bears.

After several minutes, hotel guests, suddenly aware that "Michaeo" was tossing teddy bears from the top floor, decided they wanted a souvenir themselves and joined the melee. It was an outright free-for-all. Finally, the cops arrived and broke it up. I remember the cops leading two or three girls off to jail. One was bleeding from the nose and another had an already-swelling black eye. Some were so battered and bruised they looked like they'd been in a boxing match. Those teenage girls were prepared to die to get one of "Michaeo's" teddy bears.

Epiphany

I had grown up with Bob Hope. When I was a child growing up in North Alabama in the late forties, I was an avid reader of Bob Hope comic books. On late night TV, I had watched most of the movies he had made with Bing Crosby

Thanks, PG!

and others, and in 1976 when I was working in Washington, I met him for the first time.

I was sitting in the *Insider* office in the National Press Building one afternoon when a man popped his head in the door.

"Bob Hope is down in the press room if anybody wants to interview him," he said.

I knew I had to meet the great man.

For almost an hour, several other reporters and I posed questions about his personal life and his career, but all we got back were snappy wisecracks designed to produce belly laughs rather than copy. Later, when I worked in Hollywood, I would occasionally see him in Palm Springs at his famous golf tournament or at local restaurants.

Here was a man who, in my opinion, had conquered every frontier of show business. Radio, television, vaudeville, stage, movies, singing, dancing, standup comedy, and his legendary Christmas Tours for serviceman overseas. He was truly "Mr. Show Business," entertaining Americans for generations. From alpha to omega, this man had not only bedazzled the world, but he had done so in spades.

In the early fall of 1994, I was on assignment in Palm Springs when I stopped by a Long's Drugstore to buy some toothpaste. As I started in, I saw a man walking toward me, his arm locked in the arm of another much older man to keep him erect. The older man was unshaven, wearing a baseball cap, and appeared to be slightly palsied. As I approached the pair, I could see that the older man was Bob Hope.

For a moment, I stared at the two men moving hop-step across the parking lot, the halting steps of the older man following stride-by-stride of the younger man. As I watched, I felt deep sadness. *Great God!* I thought. *Is this all that life is worth?* Here was a man who had bedazzled the entire world and now he required another human being to assist him in remaining erect. *Is that all life was worth?*

Somehow, I suddenly had a deep understanding that no matter who you are or what you have accomplished in life, this was your ultimate end. I remember thinking, there's no justice or mercy or goodness on this earth, only despair and nothingness in the end. As always, at times like these, I felt that if I had been more of a religious man, such moments wouldn't have overtaken me with such a pervasive sadness.

Chapter 15

Assignment of a Lifetime

For years, I had dreamed of being assigned a personal story for PG. John Harris had told me many times about the personal story he did for PG when he went searching the world for paradise. Once on assignment with British reporter David Wilson, he regaled me about the time he'd been dispatched to England to discover what truly happened at the Battle of Balaclava when the 600 horsemen of the famous Light Brigade were slaughtered due to a communications mix-up.

Another time, while on assignment in Virginia with Joe Webb, he related the story of how he'd spent almost a month in Quebec and London researching the death of James Wolfe, the victorious British general at the Battle of Quebec. PG wanted to know if it were true that Wolfe, as he lay dying during the raging battle, had actually said he would give up all of his military victories to have written the poem "Elegy Written in a Country Churchyard" by Thomas Gray. Joe, after his research, said it wasn't true Wolfe had made the statement as he was dying, but several nights before the battle, he had read the poem to his officers and quipped, "Gentlemen, I would rather have written that poem than take Quebec tomorrow."

PG's personal stories were never printed in the *Insider*. These were historical questions whose answers were purely for PG's own intellectual edification.

To be assigned a personal story for PG was not only a great honor, but it was a dream story, a story of a lifetime. Such stories were always assigned to top-level reporters in good standing. Simon theorized that to be assigned a personal story for PG was a reward for long years of dedicated service. Personally, I never thought I would ever actually get such an assignment, but in my heart of hearts, it was a secret dream.

In the spring of 1992, word was buzzing around the office that PG had been reading widely about the Far East. On his desk, editors had observed books about the Feudal System in Japan, the Chinese Han Dynasty, and the origins of Korean poetry.

One afternoon in late June of 1992, Simon called and said the executive editor mentioned at the meeting that day PG was planning a personal story in the next few weeks. He asked if I was interested.

"Hell, yes!!" I blurted out. "You know I'm interested."

"I'll run it up the flagpole," he said. "You realize there are no guarantees."

"I realized long ago there are no guarantees about anything at the *Insider*," I replied.

He laughed and said goodbye.

Over the next few weeks, I never mentioned the subject again, but deep within my soul, I wished with all my might that it would come true.

Then, one afternoon in late July, Simon called.

"You lucky dog," he said when I answered.

"What are you talking about?" I asked.

"You've been assigned PG's personal story," he blurted out.

I was beside myself. "What's the assignment?"

Thanks, PG!

"You're going to China to do a story about Chiang Kai-Shek."

"Holy Christ!" I said happily. "What's the angle?"

"Not sure yet," he said. "I'll have full details tomorrow."

I had to calm myself down. "When do I leave?"

"A week from Wednesday. The travel desk is putting together the arrangements now."

I was absolutely giddy with delight.

"You lucky dog," he said again. "You lucky, lucky dog! I'd give my right arm for an assignment like that."

The following morning, I received the full lead sheet.

PG wanted to know why Chiang Kai-Shek, the leader of mainland China from 1926 until 1948, didn't have any children with Madame Chiang. In 1927, Chiang had married Soong May-ling, a younger sister of Sun Yat-Sen's wife. The marriage was seen as a political move by Chiang and, in winning her hand, he promised her mother he would convert to Christianity.

In short, the marriage was to be a melding of the old—the Sun Yat-Sen legacy and the new represented by Chiang—into a powerful new political alliance. PG said the new alliance of the two leaders was merged with the marriage, but could only have been firmly cemented with the birth of a child. There had been rumors that Madame Chiang had miscarried a child, but this was never confirmed and appeared to be a publicity ploy by Chiang supporters. PG postulated that, if Chiang and Sun Yat-Sen's sister-in-law had had a child, it would have been recognized as a symbolic cementing of the old and the new and bought the two factions solidly together.

Instead, a young poet and communist named Mao Tse-Dung arose as Chiang's political rival. Not only did he challenge Chiang for the supreme leadership of China, but, with his armies, chased Chiang and his bedraggled troops across the length of the nation and finally to the island of Formosa.

"A child between them could have brought the nation together and changed the course of history," PG wrote in the lead sheet.

PG had a contact at an Asian Studies Foundation in San Francisco who said the secret lay with a woman in China who was one of Chiang's former concubines. The contact said this woman lived deep in the foothills of the Himalayan Mountains near the Tibetan-Chinese border. My contact for the story was a woman named Weiying Bi, the granddaughter of this concubine, who lived in Mianyang, China in Sichuan province. My job was to meet Weiying, travel deep into the Himalayan Mountains with her, and interview her grandmother. As I finished reading the lead sheet, my heart was already pounding with excitement.

That afternoon, I went to the UCLA library and started reading everything I could about Chiang. I scoured books about his childhood, his rise within the Chinese military, his early political maneuvering within the Kuomintang, the Chinese National Party, and, with the death of Sun Yat-Sen in 1925, his being named China's nominal leader in 1926.

My itinerary called for me to fly from LA to Beijing, then to Mianyang, where I would meet Weiying. Simon said, according to the source, Weiying spoke some English, but if I needed to, I could hire a translator. When I boarded the plane, I decided I would cross that bridge once I met my contact.

The flight from LA to Beijing was twenty-one hours. Never had I been on a single flight so long. At the Beijing airport, two Chinese security agents pulled everything out of my carry-on bag, inspected each individual item, and finally, with their stamp of approval, I boarded a flight for Mianyang.

At the Mianyang airport, I was greeted by my contact. In her early forties, Weiying was tall and thin and had a beautiful,

Thanks, PG!

high cheek-boned Asian face. I sensed a shyness, a mysterious reserve about her that immediately attracted me.

"My English is fair," she said during the cab ride to the hotel, "but there may be times when we need a translation device. We should buy one in case we need it."

I had obtained almost one thousand yuan at the LA airport, and I gave her 600 to buy the device. As we rode quietly to the hotel, out of the corner of my eye, I could see that she was intermittently checking me out. Suddenly, I turned and my eyes met hers. I could see in her eyes that she was interested in more than my journalistic ability.

From the moment I got off the plane, everything around me was a visual feast. In downtown Mianyang, the traffic was an absolute madhouse. There were no traffic lights, and cars, bicycles, three-wheeled bicycles, motor scooters, and trucks, horns blaring constantly warning other drivers to get out of the way, jammed the narrow streets. Drivers were constantly cursing, shaking their fists, and making obscene gestures. This was my first glimpse into the topsy-turvy world of China.

Finally, we arrived at the hotel. I checked into my room and Weiying said she was going to buy the translation device. By the time I had unpacked and showered, Weiying had returned with the translation device and wanted to show me how it worked. It was a hand-held device that could translate the ideograms of Mandarin Chinese into English and vice versa. I could type English characters, then push a button, and the screen would produce Chinese ideograms. To reply, she drew ideograms on the screen, then punched a button, and the screen produced English text. It was clever.

I was seated at a small desk and, as she bent over me to point out the keys, I could smell a mild hint of jasmine in her hair. I tried to follow her explanations in broken English, but the lust in our hearts was stronger than the mission at hand, and, with no words, comments, or explanations, we were instantly kissing, fondling, and undressing one another. Moments later, I was in my birthday suit and she was down to her panties.

I started for the bed.

"Close the curtains," she said.

"We're thirteen stories up," I replied.

"Close the curtains," she said again.

I closed the curtains. A woman and her modesty were at stake.

That night, she explained that the following morning, we'd be taking a bus from Mianyang to Jiuhaigao high in the Himalayas, then we'd proceed to Songpan where we'd hire a Tibetan guide to take us to Two Bamboo Mountain where her grandmother lived. She explained that we should travel as light as possible because the last leg of the journey was up a treacherous mountain trail.

"It's almost a mile up the trail and a suitcase gets heavy toward the end," she said. "Also, we'll be at 11,000 feet."

Weiying said, as a child, she had made the trip to Two Bamboo Mountain with her mother many times, but after her mother passed, she had visited her grandmother only once.

Jiuhaigao, a popular tourist destination, was dotted with small hillside villages and dozens of yellow, blue, green, and turquoise-colored lakes. The lakes, known to locals as "Sons of the Sea," took their vivid colors from rare algae that lived on the bottom.

During a bathroom break just outside of Jiuhaigao, my eyes fell upon a sprawling, aqua-blue lake that stretched into the higher, snow-capped mountains beyond. Placed prominently in front of the lake was a sign in Mandarin, which depicted a Chinese mother holding the body of a dead infant.

I turned to Weiying. "What does that say?"

She looked at me with that mysterious smile of hers. I could see she was hesitant to answer.

Thanks, PG!

"Are you sure you want to know?"

"Yes," I said.

She read the Mandarin text. "Please don't drown your baby daughter in our lake," she said.

I was shocked.

"Chinese mothers want sons, not daughters," she said, explaining that two out of every five girls born in China were murdered by their mothers, usually by drowning.

"That's terrible," I said.

"That's China," she said stoically.

The trip from Jiuhaigao to Songpan revealed a host of sights that few westerners see. In Huanglong, we stopped to eat. At a nearby construction site, I watched a group of forty to fifty men, their backs bent at forty-five-degree angles, carrying fresh earth in woven baskets from a nearby quarry to the building site. One by one, in a constant procession, the men would stop at the quarry, where a worker would shovel ten to twelve shovelfuls of dirt into the woven basket. Each worker, bent and supporting the load with a headband, would then trudge some one hundred yards to the building site, dump the basket of dirt, then return to the quarry to have the basket refilled.

All of the workers were permanently bent over from carrying the dirt-filled baskets for so many years. One could see that the supervisor of the operation had once carried baskets himself. As he walked around the site barking orders, his back was permanently bent from many years doing the same work. Never in my entire life had I seen such an operation.

Once we'd eaten, the bus churned higher into the mountains and, an hour later, we stopped at an official-looking roadside station that was flying the Chinese flag.

"This is where we get the altitude medicine," Weiying said. "We should buy two or three extras in case we need them."

Moments after we stopped, a young Chinese woman dressed in medical garb boarded the bus and began selling small vials of a brown liquid. We bought one each and gulped it down, then bought three extras for later.

For two more hours, the bus climbed higher and higher up the mountain inclines, then wound through the treacherous mountain gorges to a high point where I could see the outskirts on a major city in the distance. Songpan, a bustling beehive of gaily-painted buildings, street vendors, and horse-drawn carts, was our next stop.

Weiying said there was a small hotel she knew that was clean and reasonable and usually had hot water. It was a welcome relief to get off the bus and stretch my legs. Finally, after walking several blocks, we found the hotel and, following some ten minutes of haggling between Weiying and an old Chinese woman, we settled in for the night.

The following morning, suitcases in hand, we took a taxi from the outskirts of Songpan to a flat, grassy expanse bordered by the Lin Pi River where several hundred families of Tibetan nomads were camped. Weiying said these people, with their stoic, sunburned faces and colorful costumes, were there to graze their horses, yaks, sheep, and goats for the summer. As she and I walked among them, the children and many of the adults stared curiously at me as if I were a creature from another planet. Finally, after being sent to three separate people, Weiying negotiated a price of twenty-five yuan for one of them to take us by horse-drawn cart to Two Bamboo Mountain.

The first few miles of the journey along an unpaved, often washed-out dirt road was anything but comfortable. The apples and fresh blackberries Weiying had bought in Songpan helped ease the discomfort of the bumpy ride. Finally, around four in the afternoon, we reached the base of Two Bamboo Mountain. Weiying asked the cart driver, an early fortyish

Thanks, PG!

man with piercing eyes and wearing a black furry hat, if he could take us up the mountain trail.

His response was a quick "no." He said the narrow, rocky pass up the mountain was too dangerous. The horse could stumble in the loose rocks and we could be thrown to our deaths into the valley below. We got out of the cart, Weiying paid him, and we started walking up the narrow mountain trail.

Finally, after more than an hour's climb, we reached a small meadow clearing in the mountains. Lush with fresh green grass and a small, crystal-clear stream, I saw two dwellings. The smaller was little more than a canvas hut. Uncut stones had been stacked atop one another to form walls and a large canvas material, thrown over the top, served as a roof. The other, where Weiying's grandmother lived, was built of cut stones and formed a small rectangle with a neatly constructed wooden door and roof.

Beyond the huts, I could see a small garden and a pen with several pigs lazing in the afternoon mountain air. Behind the grandmother's hut, the mighty Himalayans rose higher and higher while in front, the foothills descended to the valley below.

I watched as Weiying started toward the canvas hut. As she approached, an elderly Chinese woman suddenly emerged and, immediately recognizing Weiying, rushed to greet her. For several moments, they chatted amiably in Mandarin, then Weiying escorted her over to meet me. I offered my outstretched hand, but she stopped several feet from me and performed the traditional Asian bow. God only knew how old this woman was! Her face was seared with deep wrinkles, she had not more than four or five teeth, and, without glasses, she squinted with difficulty to look at me.

Weiying explained that this woman was Yong-Si, her grandmother's sister. Yong-Si said her sister had gone off into the mountain to gather firewood, wild yams, and goji berries and wouldn't return until the following morning.

"We'll spend the night in her hut," Weiying said.

Inside the hut, we found heavy yak robes thrown on the dirt floor for a bed. There was a small cast-iron wood stove for cooking and heating. A large, flat stone served as a table and a small wooden bench served as a couch.

Weiying announced that she would prepare our evening meal.

"I make the best yak butter tea in all of southwest China," she said. "My grandmother taught me."

I watched as she took yak butter, tea, salt, and water and placed it in a small earthen churn.

"Are we going to check our sexual coordination again tonight?" she asked as she began churning.

I nodded.

She smiled.

Fifteen minutes later, she removed the churn lid, dipped a cupful of the pulpy froth, and handed it to me.

"You like?" she asked.

I took a sip. It wasn't bad. It had a taste similar to a salty lassi, a popular drink served in LA's Indian restaurants, except there was more of a buttery taste.

As I sipped the tea, Weiying went to a small cabinet, searched around within a pile of leaves and straw grass, and finally withdrew four preserved eggs. After two preserved eggs and a double handful of dried goji berries, I was sated. Outside, I could see that night had fallen.

"Come on," I said. "Let's feel the night air," and started for the door.

She grabbed my arm and I turned.

"No," she replied earnestly. "Let us speak to the love god first."

Thanks, PG!

Some thirty minutes later, butt-naked and our lust satisfied, we ventured outside into the darkness.

Oh, God, how can I describe the scene awaiting us? To the west, a full moon glowed golden and magnificent atop the snow-capped mountains. The night air was sweet with a soft, gentle breeze and, somewhere in the distance, I could hear the faint call of what sounded like an eagle. I thought this must be the most wonderful, glorious moment of my life. For some five minutes, we stood naked, holding hands and basking in the moonlit magnificence of the mountains.

"I'm getting cold," she said finally.

Back inside the hut, we curled up in the yak robes and chatted. She said her father had been a lower-ranking officer in the Chinese army and had been killed in a border skirmish with Tibetan rebels eight years earlier. Before his death, her father had obtained work for her at a munitions factory near Chengdu, designing and manufacturing rocket-propelled grenades. She was forty-four, divorced, and had a daughter studying medicine in Xian. Finally, when I drifted off to sleep that night, I dreamed that I was a handsome prince who had wooed and won the hand of the fair maiden.

Around ten a.m. the following morning, Yong-Si came to the door, shouting in Mandarin. When we emerged, she pointed into the distance and we could see an elderly woman, bent over and moving slowly from a heavy load, coming up the trail from the valley below.

"Let's go help her," Weiying said.

As we approached, the old woman recognized Weiying immediately, threw down the load, and ran to embrace her. She kept kissing her granddaughter again and again. Finally, when her greetings were finished, Weiying introduced me.

The woman, thin and wiry, had to be at least ninety years old. Like her sister, she had only a few visible teeth, her back was permanently bent from heavy loads, and the deep wrinkles in her face testified to too many years of hardship and worry.

Once we had helped her into her home with the load, Weiying explained why we were there and we sat down for the interview. Weiying had a list of the questions I had provided and knew exactly what the ultimate goal of the interview was.

I sat quietly nearby as Weiying conducted the interview. The old woman's face was animated, and her eyes darted happily about as she recalled her past. As Weiying would ask a question, she would pause to reflect, then carefully answer with precision and deliberation. At times, she would laugh and show only two or three teeth. At one point, she turned her face in shame away from her granddaughter. Finally, after almost an hour, Weiying stopped asking questions. I couldn't wait to hear the answers.

"She said the great general didn't have children with Madame Chiang because he was incapable of having children," Weiying started.

"He could have children," I replied. "Mao, the woman he was legally married to, bore him a son."

"That's true," she replied, "but in later years, he contracted a sexually transmitted disease from his younger concubine and, after that, could no longer father children."

"What was the disease?" I asked.

"She's not going to know something that," Weiying said. "You Americans throw around medical terms like dishwater. She's a simple woman."

"Maybe you're right," I said. "How did he contract the disease from the younger concubine?"

"As you know, the relationship between a man and his concubine was for a lifetime. In some cases, there would be years between the times the man and his concubine would be

Thanks, PG!

together. This was what happened between the great general and Yao."

"Please explain," I said.

"During one long period of the general's absence, Yao ran up huge gambling debts to some bad men and had to go work in Chengdu as a night woman to pay off the debts."

"A night woman is a prostitute?"

She nodded.

"And she caught the disease while working to pay off the debts?"

"Yes," Weiying said. "Then, almost a year later, the great general came to visit her. Although doctors cured the disease, they said he could no longer have children."

Now it became clear. I knew PG, being a physician, was going to want to know what the disease was.

"Can you ask her what the disease was?"

"I can try," she replied.

She turned to her grandmother and started speaking in Mandarin.

The old woman, her eyes clear with understanding, answered immediately.

"*Lin bing,*" she said quickly.

Weiying's eyes lit up with surprise.

"It was gonorrhea."

"Great!" I said. "How does she know all of this?"

I knew that would be the first thing PG would ask.

"She was friends with Yao for many years," Weiying said. "The concubines shared stories with one another about their relationships with the great general."

That was my story.

Two hours later, we were walking back down the rocky trail to the base of Two Bamboo Mountain. The trek back down was much easier than going up. About halfway down, I suddenly couldn't breathe. I sat in the middle of the trail.

Everything was spinning around me, and I could feel myself blacking out. I could sense my consciousness fading in and out from the shortness of breath.

Several moments later, I faded back to reality and Weiying was sitting in the middle of the trail holding my head in her lap. She held one of the vials of anti-altitude medicine to my lips.

"Drink! Drink!" she said.

For a moment, I raised my lips to the vial and drank the bitter-tasting chemical. I was still woozy, but I could feel my senses returning again.

"Rest for a few moments," she said with a motherly tone. "Your body will take the medicine and you'll breathe normally again."

She was right. Quickly, I could feel my breathing returning to normal.

Finally, after some five minutes, I got up and we continued down the trail.

"At the base of the mountain, there's a farmer," she said. "If he's at home, he'll take us back to Songpan."

Almost an hour later, we arrived at the base of the mountain, then walked several hundred yards until we reached a small farm with some twenty to thirty yaks grazing in a pasture. Weiying stood at the front gate and called out in Mandarin. Moments later, a middle-aged, Tibetan-looking man appeared. Weiying explained our needs. For a long moment, he examined me curiously, then, satisfied I wasn't dangerous, turned to Weiying, smiled, and said in Mandarin that he would take us to Songpan for twenty yuan.

Late that afternoon, we arrived back at the nomad encampment on the outskirts of Songpan. After Weiying paid the man for his services, we caught a taxi back to downtown Songpan and, thirty minutes later, we were on a bus bound for

Thanks, PG!

Mianyang. Late that night, we arrived back at the hotel. This would be our last night together.

The following morning at the airport, we said our goodbyes. We both cried as we hugged one another for the last time. Our great adventure was at an end. As I boarded the plane, I turned one last time to see her. She waved, wiped away tears, and gave me that slight, mysterious smile of hers. I knew she was remembering those precious moments we stood naked together in the moonlight atop Two Bamboo Mountain.

Some thirty-six hours later, I arrived back at LAX. Once I was back at my apartment in Sherman Oaks, I filed the story and called Simon.

"Good job, mate," he said. "The boss will be happy."

I knew I had accomplished everything PG had wanted, but I didn't get any feedback until three years later. I didn't expect an immediate response, but I had hoped he would say something. Maybe I was looking for a pat on the back. As for the trip itself, it was unforgettable.

No other story in my entire journalistic career could ever come close to my adventure into the Himalayas, knowing and loving Weiying, and witnessing the topsy-turvy work of the Chinese. As Simon said, it was an assignment of a lifetime.

Chapter 16

Trial of the Century

In Los Angeles County, Santa Monica Boulevard heads due east from the palisades overlooking the ocean through Santa Monica, West Los Angeles, Beverly Hills, and Century City. A few miles east of Santa Monica in an upscale area known as Brentwood, there is a quiet residential street called South Bundy Drive. It was here at 875 South Bundy Drive in June of 1994 that a double murder occurred, which would not only launch one of the most bizarre cultural phenomena in American history, but change the course of American journalism forever.

Orenthal James Simpson, known as O.J. or "The Juice" to millions of football fans, was a true American hero. The handsome, athletic, highly dynamic black man, born and raised in a poor area of San Francisco called Potrero Hills, was living the American Dream. His athletic ability had won him a full football scholarship to USC, where he won the prestigious Heisman Trophy. Upon graduation, he moved to a stellar pro career as one of the fastest running backs in the history of the sport, and he later became a successful TV sports commentator, pitchman, and actor. Most of all, he had won respect and public admiration across racial lines, becoming a beloved figure and role model for many.

Like many famous men in his position, there was also a dark side to our hero. He was a womanizer, had an explosive temper, especially with the women in his life, and rumors of domestic abuse constantly hung around him. At thirty-seven, he had divorced his first wife, who had been his high school sweetheart. Actually, he had "traded her for a new model," Nicole Brown, a nineteen-year-old beauty from a well-to-do Orange County, California family, who was working as a waitress at a trendy Beverly Hills nightclub. Once he met Nicole, he actually pressured the first wife to move out of the home he always referred to as "my house" and, as soon as wife #1 and their two young kids were out the door, he moved in Nicole. Their relationship was stormy from the get-go; he was jealous, controlling, and had a temper that exploded in fits of rage and jealousy.

O.J. and Nicole would eventually be married on February 2, 1985 and have two children. To say the marriage was rocky would be a supreme understatement. Only a week after the wedding, neighbors called police after hearing O.J. shouting threats and obscenities at his wife. Her family saw her black eyes, bruised face, and lacerated arms. Over the course of the marriage, the LAPD recorded a total of sixty-two separate incidents of domestic abuse—physical or mental—by O.J. against Nicole.

Finally, in the spring of 1992, the pair separated and were divorced on October 15, 1992. Nicole cited abuse and adultery and claimed that the domestic violence had begun as early as 1987.

At first, the divorce was amicable. O.J. purchased the South Bundy condo for Nicole and they talked frequently on the telephone about finances, arranging for parental visits and the education and welfare of their two children. It seemed that they both had moved on; O.J. dating a famous Victoria's Secrets model and Nichole dating various new suitors.

In late May of 1994, two weeks before she was killed, O.J. learned that Nicole was having an affair with another younger and famous football player whose life had been a virtual replica of his own. Like O.J., he was handsome, intelligent, and well spoken. Also, like O.J., he had excelled as a star running back in both college and the pros. One sports magazine described him as "the new O.J."

According to a close friend, when O.J. heard the news, he flew into a rage and called his ex-wife.

"What are you doing dating him?" the source quoted O.J. as saying. "You're making me look like a has-been. I'm telling you now to never date him again!"

Nicole calmly replied that they were divorced now and she could date whomever she pleased, just like he was doing. When she hung up, the enraged O.J. could see he no longer had the control over her he'd had during their marriage. Now she was about to do irreparable harm to not only his reputation, but his macho image as well.

Around ten p.m. on the night of June 12, 1994, O.J. went to Nicole's condo to continue the argument. What happened next is a matter of much speculation, but, according to trial records, this is what happened.

Did O.J. bring a knife? Or like he told a friend many years later, "If she had not answered the door holding a knife, she would still be alive." Whatever the origins of the knife might have been, we do know Nicole ended up dead, her throat slashed, almost decapitated inside the narrow front entrance to the condo. Before O.J. could make his escape through the narrow side passage, Ron Goldman, a waiter at the nearby Mezzaluna Restaurant where Nicole, her children, and parents had an early dinner that night, walked in to deliver the reading glasses Nicole's mom had left at the restaurant.

The two men struggled, the athlete in top shape quickly overpowering the younger man. Then he stabbed Goldman numerous times and left his bloody body in the bushes just a few feet from Nicole. The young man had not died because

Thanks, PG!

O.J. was jealous, but because he would have been a witness to the crime.

O.J. then made his way back around the side of the complex to the alley where he had parked his car and drove back to his home on Rockingham Avenue, less than a mile away, to get ready for the limo that was picking him up to drive him to LAX for a planned trip to Chicago.

In the entire history of American journalism, there was never a more perfect tabloid story than the murder of Nicole Simpson and Ron Goldman. It had every element that a good tabloid story requires. There was celebrity, glamour, wealth, sex, infidelity, intrigue, violence, drugs, and, best of all, a bloody murder. Few subjects tickle the strings of the human heart quite like murder. Of course, these observations were not lost on PG. Five days before the trial was to begin, I got a call from Simon.

"The boss has spoken," he started.

"What are you talking about?" I asked.

"PG wants you taken off celebrity coverage to cover the O.J. trial."

At first, I wasn't sure I had heard right.

"I haven't covered a murder trial in over twenty years," I objected.

"No matter, mate," he said. "God has spoken. He sent a memo to McDonald saying he wanted 'the tall guy from Tennessee' to cover the O.J. trial."

I knew there was nothing I could do.

"Take the afternoon off," Simon said consolingly. "Tomorrow, go to the crime scene, check out O.J.'s house in Brentwood, try to develop some sources in the LAPD, and start reading everything you can about O.J. We've got to immerse ourselves in this story."

The following morning, I started laying the groundwork. I went to the crime scene on Bundy Drive. Although the LAPD had tried to clean up the blood, huge splotches remained on the walkway, and even larger ones trailed along the side of the building to the rear gate. O.J. had been literally soaked in blood when he fled. I walked the two blocks down Bundy to San Vicente Boulevard to the Mezzaluna Restaurant where Ron Goldman worked, then back along the side street to Nicole's apartment, the exact route Goldman had walked only minutes before his death.

Afterward, I drove to the Rockingham home, taking what I believed was the same route O.J. used during his escape. That afternoon, I sent a detailed description of the crime scene to Simon.

"Good job with the memo," he said. "One more thing. PG wants transcripts of the entire trial for our archives. Call the court reporting company and give them your credit card."

"Where am I going to put them?" I asked.

"At your flat," he replied. "It can't be that much."

I didn't answer.

"This is going to be the mother of all feeding frenzies," he said.

"I think you're right," I replied.

On January 24, 1995, the first day of the trial, I drove from my apartment in the Valley the eighteen miles to Los Angeles Superior Court in downtown LA. When I emerged from underground parking and started walking up Hill Street, the circus-like atmosphere that would characterize the entire trial was already in full swing. Homeless black men lazed on the sidewalk displaying crudely drawn signs that proclaimed, "Free O.J.!" Street vendors hawked T-shirts shouting, "Cut the Juice Loose!" Baseball caps with the words "Free O.J.!" were for sale. There were bracelets, necklaces, and breast pins reiterating the same theme.

As I neared the courthouse entrance, I was greeted with an overflow crowd of rowdy spectators, television crews, and

Thanks, PG!

print and TV journalists from all over the world and a whole host of curiosity-seekers who were there only to say they had been there. From that very first day, I could see that the entire episode was destined to become everything but a murder trial.

From the very first gavel blow, the proceedings lived up to its billing as the "Trial of the Century." The lead prosecutor was an attractive, leggy, brunette divorcee. Her assistant was a bald-headed, bespectacled black man, apparently chosen because the prosecution expected race to be a factor in the trial. On the defense side, the amount of sheer lawyering had to be an undeniable world record.

In American jurisprudence, there is no standard number of lawyers a defendant can have to represent him. In murder trials, most defendants never have more than two or three. In this case, a single defendant had fifteen lawyers who represented the most prestigious names in the profession. Even further, the defense had hired a troupe of its own DNA, blood, and forensics experts. Already, the jury and the world were being set up for insurmountable information overload.

Every day for the next ten months, I sat in the media feed room next door to the courtroom and listened to testimony, the eternal jockeying by attorneys, the endless swearing-ins, and the interminable drone of witnesses' testimony. There was the barking dog, Kato Kaelin's thumps in the night, the blood and fiber evidence, the limo driver's testimony, Mark Fuhrman's use of the N-word, and charges by the defense that the LAPD not only mishandled evidence, but actually planted evidence against O.J. In many cases, the testimony of a single witness would drone on for five or six days.

Over the course of the trial, I became friends with reporters from several local newspapers as well as local television. One of these was Jim Chambliss, a cameraman for a Santa Barbara TV station. With long hair, glasses, and a quiet manner, Jim was in his early forties, and his appearance harked back to the seventies when tie-dyed T-shirts, candle-making, and Pink Floyd was the rage. A native of Pasadena, he had moved to Ventura County as an adult to pursue his passion for surfing. Over lunch, he explained that he was on probation with the station.

"What happened?" I asked.

"The company has a strict policy against inter-office romances," he said. "I was dating one of the assistant producers. Although we tried to keep it a secret, we got caught."

"How long is your probation?"

"Three months."

"Good luck!" I said.

Every Monday, a stack of the previous week's court transcripts were delivered to the door of my apartment and, once I retrieved them, I stored them in the closet in my spare bedroom. As the stacks of court documents grew higher and higher, I wondered how the jury was going to wrap their heads around these thousands and thousands of pages. By early May, my closet was more than half full of court transcripts.

In mid-June, the trial took a decisive, fatal turn. In their investigation, LAPD investigators had found one black leather glove at the crime scene and its match at Simpson's Rockingham home. According to the prosecution, the glove from the crime scene contained DNA evidence from our hero as well as the two victims.

On the morning of June 15, 1995, the prosecution asked Simpson to try on the glove. When O.J. tried to slip the glove on his right hand, it was obvious to the jury and the world that the glove didn't fit. It was far too small for his much larger hand. From that moment forward, the jury's decision was a done deal and the lead defense attorney, Johnnie Cochran, kept the episode fresh in the minds of the jury for the remainder of the trial.

Thanks, PG!

"If it don't fit, you must acquit!" he kept saying over and over as if it was an advertisement for a soft drink or laundry detergent.

On Monday of the following week, when I arrived at the courthouse, I saw Jim, my friend with the Santa Barbara TV station, waiting outside the courtroom.

"Got a minute?" he asked.

"Sure," I replied.

"I got something I want you to see."

We went into the feed room where he had a video replay machine. As I took a seat, he popped a tape into the machine and the images began to whirl past. Finally, he stopped the footage at a point dated June 14, one day before the glove incident.

"Look at this," he said. "This is test footage I ran on June 14 just to make sure everything was working okay."

The opening images showed the glove on the exhibit table. Moments later, the defense attorney could be seen walking over to the exhibit table, examining the glove, trying it on, then replacing it on the table.

"So what's the point?" I asked.

He rolled the footage back to the beginning.

"Look closely at the glove before he tried it on," Jim said. "You can see the edge of the lining."

I looked closely and, sure enough, I could see the furry edges of a lining inside the glove. He rolled the tape forward and showed the glove after the lead defense attorney had tried it on. I could no longer see the lining.

"Holy Christ," I replied. "The glove wouldn't fit because the defense attorney pushed the lining up into the fingers when he tried it on."

"Looks that way!" Jim said finally.

"That could change the course of the trial," I said. "You've got to show that to the judge."

Jim looked at me, then removed the tape and turned off the video player.

"What are you going to do with that tape?"

"I'm not sure yet," he said.

Moments later, the trial was beginning for the day and Jim hustled out of the feed room into the courtroom.

All that night, I kept thinking about the footage. From all indications, the lead defense attorney had tampered with evidence. I couldn't wait to talk to Jim the next morning.

"What did you do with that footage?" I asked when I saw him.

"It's gone!" he said.

"Gone?" I replied, shocked at hearing the words. "What do you mean, gone?"

"I destroyed it," he said. "I don't want to do anything to draw attention to myself. I'm going to keep my head low until this probation is over."

"You could change the course of the trial of the century," I replied.

"I'm not looking for fame or fortune," he said. "All I want is to keep my job."

I shook my head in disbelief.

I considered telling Simon what Jim had uncovered; however, I knew if I did, he would tell PG and all the stops would have been removed to retrieve the footage. PG would have offered millions for something like that.

The trial dragged on for another four months. The information overload was astounding, and I watched as the trial transcripts kept piling up. By late August, the closet was full, and I moved the bed out of my spare bedroom so there would be more space for the transcripts. I kept thinking, how in the world is the jury supposed to wrap their heads around this much evidence? One would need a team of college

Thanks, PG!

researchers to sift through that stack of files and make any logical sense out of it.

By early September, the trial started to affect me mentally. My mind was becoming a whirling dervish of images and names derived from the trial. Names like Vannatter, Clark, Fuhrman, Ito, Shapiro, Darden, and Cochran suddenly started popping into my mind at the most unexpected moments. I'd be driving home after a day's testimony and would hear Marcia Clark or Robert Shapiro or Johnny Cochran's voice droning on and on.

It even affected my dreams. One of my fondest memories of childhood was going fishing with my father at a small creek near our house. Our favorite fishing hole was at a wide point in the creek where a storm had blown a tree down across the creek, and my father and I would walk out on to the log, seat ourselves, and catch bream, perch, and crappie. One night, my dream world returned to those days. As I sat happily on the log, pulling in pan-sized bream, I suddenly glanced over at where my father normally sat. I was absolutely shocked. Sitting on the log beside me with a fishing pole in his hand was the lead defense attorney. I had gone fishing with Johnny Cochran. The next morning when I woke up, I knew I had been covering the O.J. trial far too long.

Finally, in late September, the defense rested, Judge Ito charged the jury and, after only four hours of deliberation, they came back with a verdict. When the "Not Guilty" verdict was announced, O.J. looked dazed, confused, and disoriented. His face had a befuddled expression that seemed to say, "*Hey, what happened? This is what I wanted, but I never dreamed it would really come true! I did the deed, but now I'm free? What happened?*"

Chapter 17

Death of PG

The last time I saw PG alive was in late December of 1995. The O.J. trial was over, Bill Clinton was president, peace accords had been signed between Bosnia, Serbia, and Croatia, and Israeli Prime Minister Yitzhak Rabin had been assassinated at a peace rally in Tel Aviv.

For the past three Christmases, Simon had asked me to come to Rosebud to participate in the opening festivities of the famous Largest Christmas Tree display. He said it was good politics to appear in the office during the Christmas holidays and remind PG that I was alive and well. That year, as I had in the past, I tried to beg off, but Simon said I really should make an appearance, so I relented. Three weeks earlier, I had broken off my relationship with a brunette in Palm Springs, and I knew it would be a lonely Christmas if I stayed in LA. In retrospect, I'm glad I did. It would be a Christmas I would always remember.

On the afternoon of Dec. 22, 1995, the plane landed at Palm Beach International just as the sun was setting. I got off the plane, went to the hotel, checked in, and then headed to the bar where I found Simon, Clive, and Bob. They were as happy to see me as I was them, and they regaled me with all of the latest *Insider* stories and gossip. Before I left, Simon and I agreed to attend the Christmas tree spectacle the following

Thanks, PG!

night. He said it was the last Saturday night before Christmas and the whole world would be there to join in the festivities.

The greatest newspaper promotion in the history of journalism was the *Insider*'s annual World's Largest Christmas tree spectacle. Every year, PG would send his minions to the northwestern US to locate the tallest fir tree they could find. Once identified, it was cut and placed on a railcar, which traveled 3600 miles to Rosebud. That year, PG had brought in a 117-foot tall monster from the backwoods near Eugene, Oregon. Once it arrived, it was decorated with more than 15,000 lights, 1600 colored basketball-sized balls, 1250 red bows, 1800 three-foot candy canes and snowflakes, topped with a six-foot lighted silver star and surrounded by elaborate animated displays and model trains.

When the tradition started in 1971, it was a huge success, and over the years, as the crowds grew, so did the height and spectacle of the tree. When the tree reached 117 feet in 1995, it was listed in the Book of World Records as the "World's Tallest Decorated Christmas Tree." Like P.T. Barnum, PG was keenly aware that people were interested in extremes such as the largest, the smallest, the widest, and the thinnest. The Christmas tree, which brings happiness to all eyes that gaze upon it, was a perfect promotional symbol for the *Insider*.

The next morning at the office, Simon handed me a lead sheet and said to try to look busy. It was an assignment about a blind Inuit Eskimo in Barrow, Alaska who hunted seals with his wife who served as his eyes. I was calling Alaska directory assistance when I heard the whistle of the Florida Central train around West Palm Beach. The minute I heard the whistle, I hung up the phone and rushed to the nearby window to see if the side door to PG's office was opening.

It was, and out came PG. He looked up the tracks and saw the train coming. As the train approached, PG was some fifteen feet from the track. The train was traveling faster than usual and, as always, PG braced for the blast of air. As the locomotive roared past, the sudden blast of air knocked PG off his feet and he went sprawling on the ground. After a few moments, he raised himself to a sitting position beside the railroad track, his thinning hair and clothes fluttering in the train-borne wind, and watched the railcars rumble past. Once he saw the caboose, he got up to his feet, dusted himself off, and started back to his office. Whether he wanted to admit it or not, PG wasn't as strong and agile as he once had been.

That evening after work, Simon and I met for drinks before heading to the *Insider* campus to see the Christmas tree. When we arrived, the employee parking lot was jammed full. Cars were parked sides along Dixie Highway two and three deep. Thousands of local residents from the nearby beach towns as well as people from as far away as Miami, Jacksonville, and Tampa were on hand to witness PG's celebration display.

With all the color and bright lights, the grounds had a certain circus atmosphere. Vendors selling popcorn, cotton candy, caramel corn, and souvenir replicas of the tree were on hand to hawk their wares. An estimated 10,000 people were milling around the grounds, which featured not only the tree, but several animated displays and advertisements for the *Insider*.

On the front lawn, two model trains had been set up. The first, the large one, contained almost 500 feet of track, which wound through the lush foliage at the *Insider* front entrance and encompassed approximately half of a football field.

The smaller track was part of a children's show, which featured PG as "Mr. Choo-Choo." Attached to the second setup was a small stage with an audience seating area and, above the stage, was a huge sign that proclaimed, "Mr. Choo-Choo."

Thanks, PG!

Simon and I could see that a small crowd was taking seats for a new show.

"Come on, mate," he said. "You got to see this."

Moments later, Simon and I were seated among some fifty to seventy-five people, mostly children and parents, when the curtain opened. On stage, we saw PG's long-time secretary Susan Castellano acting as MC. Behind her was a replica of a train engineer's console with levers and gauges and all manner of instruments required to control and operate a train. In the center of the stage was a one-foot-high model train locomotive waiting at a station labeled "Miami." Across the front and side of the locomotive were emblazoned front pages of recent *Insider* issues. Behind the console, the tracks had been elevated so the audience could see the journey of the train.

"Good evening, boys and girls," Susan said. "Thanks for coming to see Mr. Choo-Choo, the man who delivers the *National Insider* all over our nation each and every week. We hope you enjoy the show. Now I'd like to introduce Mr. Choo-Choo himself."

PG, dressed in a 1940s railroad engineer's costume complete with a blue and white striped cap, khaki shirt, overalls, and heavy work shoes, stepped out on the stage. Susan started to applaud and the crowd followed suit with raucous clapping. PG smiled his trademark smile and doffed his engineer's hat to the audience. After the applause died away, Susan continued.

"Now, Mr. Choo-Choo will take us on a journey across the USA as he delivers the *National Insider* and all of the latest news to our millions of readers," she said.

PG took a seat at the console and started the locomotive.

"Yea! Yea!" the children screamed as the replica locomotive engine fired up and left the station.

"First, we're going from Miami to New York," Susan said. "New York is the home of the New York Yankees, Central Park, the Empire State Building, and Staten Island."

As the model train made its way across Georgia, North Carolina, and Virginia, Susan coached the audience.

"Tell Mr. Choo-Choo to blow the whistle," she instructed.

"Blow the whistle!" the children screamed.

PG reached up and pulled a rope.

"Whewwww! Whewwww!" the whistle sounded and emitted several small puffs of steam with each blast.

"Yea!" the children screamed, and the toy train pulled alongside a loading platform with a New York skyline background.

The children watched as a small robotic man pushed a huge bundle of newspapers off on to the platform, then the toy train started off again.

"Now we're off to Chicago," Susan continued, "home of the Sears Tower, Wrigley Field, Lake Michigan, and the Al Capone Museum."

The children watched eagerly as the train made its way across the replica states of Pennsylvania, Ohio, and Indiana. As the train rolled out of Ohio, the crowd could see there was water across the tracks in Indiana.

"Look! Look!" Susan said urgently. "There's water on the tracks. Mr. Choo-Choo has to stop the train."

"Stop the train! Stop the train!" the children screamed.

PG pulled a lever and the train lurched to a stop, then PG reversed the train and revved the engine. With a full head of steam, it took a running go at the water. As the toy train sped through the water, splashing water on either side of the tracks, the children screamed with delight.

At the Chicago station, the little robotic man pushed a bundle of newspapers onto the loading platform and the train was off again.

Thanks, PG!

"Now we're off to Los Angeles," Susan said as the train pulled out and made its way across the heartland states en route to California.

Moments later, after making the LA "delivery," the train headed back eastward back across Arizona, New Mexico, and Texas. As the toy train approached central Texas, the children could see that toy cows were on the tracks.

"Oh, no!" Susan screamed urgently. "There are cows on the track in Texas and Mr. Choo-Choo has got to stop the train. Tell Mr. Choo-Choo to stop the train."

"Stop the train! Stop the train!" the children screamed.

PG appeared to be dozing at the console.

"Louder! Louder!" Susan urged. "Mr. Choo-Choo is napping."

"Stop the train! Stop the train!" the children screamed again, louder this time.

Suddenly, PG abruptly woke up and peered at the tracks ahead. With a surprised look, he grabbed a lever and pulled with all his might. The train lurched to a squealing stop, then he blew the whistle and the cattle slowly moved off the tracks and the locomotive was on its way again.

"Yea!" The children applauded in unison.

"Whew! That was close," Susan said. "Now Mr. Choo-Choo will bring the train back to Miami."

As the train started off again, I saw PG's face produce a smile like I had never seen before. Normally, he had his trademark know-it-all grin, but this time, it was a full, natural, ear-to-ear smile. It was the natural, glorious, satisfied smile of a man totally in his element. He was making people happy with his creations and he was truly delighted with himself and his world.

As Simon and I watched the toy train return to "Miami," I reflected that the train, in many ways, was as mindless and silly as the publication itself, but it was so much fun. No one was hurt by the silliness, and it brought joy to the hearts of the people who witnessed it. How could anyone vilify a man who only wanted to make other people happy? Once the train returned to the "Miami" station, Susan thanked the audience for attending and added that all children would receive their free foot-long candy canes upon exiting.

"He's a bloody genius," Simon said as we filed out of the seating area. "He can do anything and do it better than anyone else."

I nodded my agreement.

As we returned outside, we were watching Susan hand out the last of the candy canes when one of the company's security guards rushed over to her. The guard was explaining some problem in the parking lot. She listened, then went behind the stage and PG emerged. For a moment, PG listened to the security guard, then, after hearing the problem, he turned and started to the parking lot.

Simon and I followed.

In the parking lot, another security guard was arguing with a middle-aged man who was standing outside an old sedan.

PG stepped up.

"What's the problem?" he asked.

"This guy won't move his car," the guard said. "He says his son wants to see the Christmas tree up close."

"Please let us stay just for a few minutes," the man's wife pleaded through the car's open passenger window. "Our son has waited all year to see the tree."

"You can park over there," PG said, pointing to the empty spaces along Dixie highway. "There's plenty of room and you can walk to the tree."

"My son Timmy can't walk," the woman said.

"Can't walk?" PG said.

"Yes," she continued. "He had a rare disease as a baby and his legs and feet are so twisted he can't walk."

Thanks, PG!

PG turned from the woman to the young boy, maybe seven or eight years of age, who was peering out the open back door window.

"Please, mister," the child pleaded. "Just for a few minutes."

PG didn't answer at first. He looked thoughtfully at the parents for a moment, then back to the child.

"You really want to see the tree up close?" he asked.

"Oh, yes, sir!" the child said happily.

"It would mean so much to him," the mother said.

PG looked at the child, then turned to the mother.

"I'm Padrone Gallione, owner of the *Insider*," he said. "I'd like to personally take your son to see the tree."

"Thank you so much," the mother said. "He'll love it."

"Come on, Timmy," PG said. "We're going to see the Christmas tree."

PG leaned into the car and the child put his arms around PG's neck, then PG gently lifted the child out of the car and the security guard closed the door. In the Christmas lights, we could see that the child's legs and feet were horribly deformed. Holding the child gently and carefully in his arms, PG started for the Christmas tree. Simon and I and the child's family followed.

As we watched, PG made his way through the crowd of onlookers to the tree. Once he had reached the base, PG, cradling the child in his right arm and pointing with the other, explained about the lights and the ornaments and the candy canes. For almost twenty minutes, PG walked around the tree with the little boy in his arms. At one point, the little boy wanted to touch one of the giant colored ornaments and PG held his crippled body up to the tree so he could touch one of the ornaments.

As Simon and I watched PG holding the child up to the giant Christmas tree, the little boy's eyes glistened with happiness and excitement. Like the little boy, PG's eyes shined with pure joy, and he flashed that same satisfied smile I had seen during the "Mr. Choo-Choo" show when he pretended to be asleep at the engineer's console. It was a natural, glorious, self-satisfied smile. Somehow in my heart, I was overjoyed. I had never imagined a side like that to him. I had always seen the driving, demanding, tyrannical, deeply intellectual side of the man. Somehow, I never dreamed that, with all the weirdness and eccentricity and pure madness he was famous for, he was capable of that level of love and compassion.

When PG started back to the car with the child still in his arms, I turned to Simon. Huge tears were rolling down his cheeks.

"Sorry, mate," he said, wiping away the tears. "You know, you owe this man as much as I do."

"Yes, I do," I replied.

Finally, PG returned the child to the family car and told the mother to call ahead next year and he would do the same thing again. She said she would, then we watched as PG waved goodbye and the old sedan pulled out of the *Insider* parking lot. As the car disappeared into the darkness, PG peered after it for a long moment, then abruptly turned from the parking lot and took a seat on a nearby bench. Simon and I watched as he lit a cigarette and took a deep drag.

I wondered why a man as intelligent as PG smoked two packs of cigarettes a day, then I remembered that PG had grown up during the late twenties and early thirties, an age when America's industrial growth was in full swing. Huge manufacturing plants were belching smoke, trains, cars, and ships were emanating giant plumes of hydrocarbons, and mighty hydroelectric plants were burning coal and other fossil fuels to generate electricity for American homes and businesses. It was a time when smoke was a symbol of power and prosperity. It was a time when smoking was almost

Thanks, PG!

patriotic, and PG apparently didn't want to be left out. This love of smoke explained his love of trains.

Moments later, Simon excused himself to go to the men's room and PG looked up and saw me.

"Billy Don!" he called.

Oh, God! I thought. *Not this!*

I was deathly afraid, but I knew I couldn't ignore the call.

"Yes, sir," I said and started walking toward the bench.

"Have a seat," he said, motioning to the empty seat beside him and taking another long drag on the cigarette.

As instructed, I took a seat. As I did, I could feel my body tense with fear and nervousness.

"How do you like the tree?" he asked.

"Oh, it's great, Mr. Gallione," I replied nervously.

"Yes, it's been lots of fun," he said.

For a long moment, we sat quietly.

"You know, Billy Don, you've been an excellent reporter over the years," he said finally. "You've covered some of the biggest stories the *Insider* has published. Have I kept you on your toes?"

"Yes, sir!" I replied, fearing that he would notice that I answered everything with "Yes, sir!"

"And I loved the Chiang Kai-Shek story. Good read! Good reporting! Did you enjoy doing the story?"

"Yes, sir!" I replied.

For another long moment, we remained quiet. I could feel my shoulders trembling.

"Has it been fun?" he asked.

"Yes, sir!"

"Good!"

"Thanks, Mr. Gallione," I said. I didn't dare call him PG.

For a long moment, he was silent, then he put out the cigarette and stood.

"Well, I've got one more 'Mr. Choo-Choo' show to do," he said.

I stood with him.

"Merry Christmas, Billy Don," he said, offering his hand and flashing his trademark grin.

"Merry Christmas, Mr. Gallione," I replied, firmly shaking his hand.

As I held his hand and looked briefly into his eyes, I felt that same searching, piercing glare I knew so well and immediately turned my eyes away.

He started back to the front of the building. I was relieved as I watched him striding away.

Suddenly, he turned.

"Billy Don!" he called, walking back toward me.

Oh God! I thought. *What's he going to say this time?*

"One thing I wanted to tell you."

"Yes, sir?"

"I always knew you were from Alabama," he said. "The thing about you being from Tennessee was just a ruse."

I nodded, still unable to look into his eyes.

"I had to create an inner fear to control you," he continued. "I knew I had to present myself as weirdly wacky as possible or you would have thought you had me figured out. I couldn't let you define me or categorize me. Then all of the mysterious fear I needed would never had been created. Do you understand, Billy Don?"

"Yes, sir," I replied.

Never in my life had I said "Yes, sir!" back-to-back so many times.

"And it seems to have worked well," he continued. "You've been an excellent reporter."

"Thanks, Mr. Gallione!" I said.

"Merry Christmas again!" he said abruptly.

"Merry Christmas!" I replied.

Thanks, PG!

With a wave of the hand, he turned again and started to walk back to the front of the main building. As he walked away, I kept hearing him say "Merry Christmas!", but as I listened to his words over and over in my head, it sounded more like *Goodbye!*

*****

Back in LA, I returned to my regular routine. I put the Christmas visit to Rosebud out of my mind and returned to calling sources, creating leads, working stakeouts, searching databases, and doing my Sunday walks along the boardwalk in Venice. Despite the distractions, the issue of PG's health was never totally removed from my mind. I knew he didn't have long on this earth. Ultimately, it would be his worship of smoke that would kill him.

On the morning of April 23, 1996, PG got out of bed at his luxurious ocean-side mansion near Rosebud. He slipped on a bathrobe and told his wife he was going to the kitchen to make coffee. After she didn't hear anything for several minutes, she went to the kitchen and found him lying unconscious on the floor. He had had a massive heart attack. Local paramedics were called. He died en route to the hospital in an ambulance he had donated to the City of Rosebud.

Simon attended the funeral, expecting it to be like a mafia funeral one sees in the movies, but it was nothing like that. The service was solemn and the bulk of the attendees were friends, family, *Insider* employees, some minor celebrities, and the people PG had "made happy" over the years. Simon said he cried "like a baby" when they lowered PG's coffin into the earth. On his tombstone was inscribed the words *"He brought happiness to millions."*

*****

From a historical standpoint, it was only fitting that PG should make his exit after the O.J. trial. I always remembered the story about Mark Twain and how he was born in a year when Haley's comet passed through. He died seventy-six years later when it made its next regular pass. The O.J. trial was the death knell for PG; not only was it the finest hour for PG and the *Insider*, it was the pinnacle of power for print tabloids in America.

With the end of the O.J. trial, PG's life's work was finished. The seeds of celebrity gossip he'd planted in the seventies and watered in the eighties exploded into full bloom during the O.J. trial. After the O.J. trial, lurid stories of murder, drugs, sex, and celebrity scandal were no longer confined to tabloids. Suddenly, when mainstream publications saw how the public hungered for every word and action of the O.J. trial, similar tabloid subjects flooded print, digital, and television news media like never before. Of course, this would dampen interest in the print tabloids because readers hungry for celebrity gossip could now get their fill instantly on television, daily newspapers, and the Internet. This proliferation of tabloid content into the mainstream media wouldn't totally spell the death of the *Insider,* but the glory and power the *Insider* had enjoyed during PG's reign were gone forever.

The eccentric genius who was my hero had passed to the great beyond. As a result, it was impossible for his life's work, the *National Insider*, to not be affected by his absence. After he died, his family continued the tradition he'd established and kept the *Insider* operational for almost a year. Throughout that time, circulation remained relatively stable, then, in the summer of 1997, the family sold the *Insider* and its sister publications to a group of private investors from Wall Street.

Unlike PG, the new owners were investors and business people, not editors. During the first few months, the face of

Thanks, PG!

the publication didn't show any significant problems, but in the fall of 1997, circulation started dropping rapidly and nobody knew why. They were printing the same kinds of stories they were publishing during PG's reign. They had the same editors and reporters, the same delivery trucks, the same presses, the same everything, but circulation was falling rapidly.

The problem was that the great genius who could bestride the cutting edge of daily news and come up with just the right mix of tabloid stories for each week's final edition was missing. The magic was gone, and so was the heart and soul of the publication. It was dying on the vine.

Once circulation started falling, revenue plummeted, and as revenue went down, salaries and expenses were cut to the bone. This only exacerbated the situation. Many reporters and editors who reveled in the madness created by PG realized the heart had been ripped out of the publication.

Quickly, one by one, top editors and reporters started to leave the company. Simon was one of the first. Late one afternoon in the fall of 1997, he called.

I could hear the anguished agitation in his voice the moment he started to speak.

"What's wrong?" I asked.

"I'm packing it in, mate," he said angrily. "These new publishers are a bunch of clowns. I'm calling so you'll be the first to know."

"What are you going to do?" I asked.

"I've already done it," he said. "I gave the executive editor my resignation moments ago. The madness is gone and so am I."

After an initial burst of anger and frustration, his voice finally calmed to a rational tone. He said he had put in a lead for a story about a blind man at a Wisconsin car dealership who had sold more cars than any other car salesmen in the US.

He said the idea was approved, but the new woman editor said the story would have to be done by a stringer.

"These new blokes don't know how to run a newspaper," he said. "I miss PG."

"So do I," I said.

Simon explained that he was going back to the Lake District of England and fulfill his boyhood dream of opening a fishing tackle shop. He said his wife missed her parents in London and he missed the mountains, valleys, and lakes of his youth. I told him I understood because I was feeling the same constraints from the new administration. He said goodbye and hung up. That would be the last time I talked to Simon.

Three months later, I was dispatched to San Diego to get a story about a woman raising a love child from a member of a famous comedy duo. She lived in La Jolla and I had driven my personal car from LA to La Jolla, made five to six separate trips into San Diego and, after I finally got the interview and filed the story, drove back to the San Fernando Valley. When I added up the mileage, I had put a total of 680 miles on my car.

When I turned in the expense report, the young South African reviewing expenses said the company's new policy was that they would only pay twenty-two cents a miles for the use of personal cars. Under PG's reign, they paid thirty-five cents per mile. I flew into a rage and called my new woman editor to appeal.

"My hands are tied," she said. "The new owners are in total control of the money."

I knew that this was the end of the line, and I resigned my position two days later. It had been a good run and I could well afford it. I owned a condo in Sherman Oaks, a vacation home in Maui, and had over $650,000 in my 401K. Thanks to PG, I was able to live my retirement in the manner I had become accustomed.

Thanks, PG!

Chapter 18

In Memoriam

The world has always made fun of, sneered at, and downright vilified people it doesn't understand. In fact, the world usually won't bother to discover the truth about such people. It is far too easy to write someone off as being a renegade, a misfit, an aberration that doesn't fit into any of the recognized molds human beings use to classify their fellow man. Invariably, these people are branded "weird" or "mad" and placed off in a corner by themselves. This was the case with PG.

In many cases, renegades are relegated to their special corner of the world and forgotten. If they do manage to later succeed in their "madness," they are then heralded and revered for their contrariness and, in many cases, their rebelliousness is given as the reason for that success. In PG's case, his "madness" not only made him wildly successful, but gave rise to a totally new dimension in American journalism

PG was a true individualist who told the rest of the publishing world to kiss his "pizza." He was going to print his publication his way, and if the rest of the world didn't approve, they could go to hell. During the early experimental days of the *Insider*, PG gave the world a publication like it had never seen before. Although the content of the publication evolved over the years from a carnival sideshow into a low brow *Reader's Digest*, PG had ventured into a part of the American psyche where no other publisher had dared go. Yes, there were imitators, copycats, and naysayers, but, in the end, PG was the original. Not only did the *Insider* become successful beyond belief, but ultimately, PG was the poster child for tabloid publishing in America.

One of the dominant characteristics of PG's renegade publishing style was that he saw no need for specialization. All around him, magazines were publishing stories confined to a single topic. These included fashion, finance, boating, politics, cooking, coin collecting, and any other of the myriad subjects human beings might be interested in. PG believed that a magazine should be for everyone, not just a select few. In his heart, I believe he felt there was a certain arrogance in specialization.

As a result, he felt it was perfectly acceptable to publish a truly solid medical advice story alongside a story about some guy in the heartland who had been abducted by a UFO. Couldn't his readers use helpful medical information and, at the same time, have a sense of wonder about whether UFOs existed? In PG's mind, the two subjects weren't mutually exclusive. Or, he would print a story on how to remove stains from a tablecloth alongside a story of some guy who was almost killed by a grizzly in the backwoods of Alaska. PG had enough respect for his readers to understand that they had multiple interests. Down deep, I've always felt that PG fancied himself "a man of the people."

While the mainstream press doddered about day after day in their smug self-righteousness and their circulation remained the same year after year, the circulation of the *Insider* soared and profits went through the ceiling. His reporters and editors were the highest paid in the world and his editorial budget was limitless. That was the proof of the pudding as far as PG was concerned. PG was proving his point with profits, not hollow

Thanks, PG!

words of disdain and criticism. As always, PG's vision was far ahead of the pack.

Yes, he was tyrannical to a fault. In fact, his tyranny was legendary. People were fired for wearing the wrong color shirt, parting their hair on the wrong side, or opening a window to let in some air. One must remember that PG had a city to run. He didn't have time for underlings who wanted to question his methods or policies. If one didn't agree with the city's rules and policies, then get the hell out.

Many critics, in analyzing PG, couldn't see beyond the fact that he was Italian. They claimed that his tyranny was akin to the techniques used by a mafia godfather to enforce his will upon his underlings. They claimed he was a latter day Frank Costello, Paul Castellano, or Vito Corleone. This was pure nonsense and little more than the unbridled imagination of an uninformed mind. They also claimed that his unabashed use of money to buy stories was akin to "making him an offer he can't refuse."

None of that could be further from the truth. As for the money, I nailed down thousands of good stories by paying sources a fee. Many of these stories would never have been published if I had asked these sources to provide the information for free. Paying for information doesn't mean the source is going to intentionally lie. Like it or not, money talks in this world. The conclusion here is that there were many, many more dimensions to the man than his Italian heritage. As always, PG did things his way.

Deep inside, PG felt a need to create a mysterious inscrutability about himself for the benefit of those around him. It was a control technique. Every time someone felt he had PG figured out, PG would go out of his way to prove him wrong. He wanted to remain mysterious, inscrutable to the end. I always remember the story of the editor who, in the late seventies, had a story he was absolutely sure PG would love.

John Isaac Jones

This editor had uncovered a story about this elderly woman in a small village in Northern Italy who had put her son on a bus to go fight for Mussolini in 1938. After her son failed to return, the old woman walked from her village to the bus stop in the nearby town every day for the next thirty-odd years to see if her son got off the bus.

"It's a great story of motherly love," the editor told one of his reporters. "And, since PG is Italian, he'll love it."

PG read the lead, winced, and scratched a big X kill mark on the lead sheet.

"What a dumb broad!" he scribbled on the lead sheet. "Why didn't she take a taxi?"

Publicly, his great hero was William Randolph Hearst, but down deep inside, the spirit of the great circus showman P.T. Barnum was always alive and well. During the late sixties and early seventies, the old black and white *Insider* carried numerous stories that were little more than print versions of circus sideshows. Glaring headlines such as "I Boiled my Baby and Ate It" or "I'm Sorry I Killed My Mother but Glad I Killed My Father" were standard fare for its pages. Employees always referred to this side of PG as his "circus side." These stories were little more than experiments in the ongoing evolution of the *Insider*. In later years, these stories were toned down to headlines about the tallest or shortest person, the longest fingernails, the longest hair, most pierced and other visual extremes. To a large degree, the world has remembered PG's P.T. Barnum side rather than his Hearst side.

As a reporter for PG, one was always at the mercy of his "madness." One never knew what wild, crazy story one would be assigned on any given day, and one knew that each and every story was going to be a new adventure. In fact, one had to be a little off his rocker to work at the *Insider* and, somewhere deep inside, I felt I shared the same "madness" PG had. The uninitiated outsider couldn't imagine the wonder and

Thanks, PG!

excitement of working in such a freewheeling, unfettered environment.

Finally, if one knew PG, one couldn't help but be staggered by the largesse of his intellect. Forget that he was an engineer, a lawyer, and a physician! He was also a philosopher, a historian, and a scientist whose mind stretched across the ages.

PG could laugh in your face and retrace the history of Hannibal crossing the Alps, the ethnic composition of his armies, and their exploits on the road to Rome. PG could explain the chemical bonding techniques that occur during the fractional distillation of petroleum or give one the skinny on the legal origins of habeas corpus in a minute flat. Ask him about the Battle of Waterloo and how Wellington's forces had taken Napoleon's troops by surprise on the grassy knolls of southwest Belgium. For PG, it was a piece of cake.

This same intellect could take a run-of-the-mill news story and come up with an entirely new angle that made the story special. The true wonder of the man was that he was an endless reservoir of creative thinking who was forever searching the cutting edge of world events to find the big story. Many, many times, I've wondered why a man of such intellect would spend his life producing entertainment old and young women. His answer was, "Because it's fun."

His generosity was legendary. His reporters and editors were not only the highest paid in the world, but his lavish gift giving to the local community was beyond reproach. He bought ambulances and police cars for the City of Rosebud. He provided playing fields, equipment, and uniforms for the local Little League teams. His yearly donation to the local hospitals and medical clinics were far into the millions. He provided holiday meals and clothing for homeless people in Rosebud. For more than fifteen years, he was the largest donor to local charities not only in Rosebud, but in all of South

Florida. PG loved to make other people happy. His generosity was so lavish and so widespread that the Rosebud mayor once suggested his parents should have named him Generoso.

My most endearing memory of PG was watching him holding the little crippled boy up to touch an ornament on the Christmas tree. I'll never forget the extraordinary look of happiness in the child's eyes and the wonderful glow in PG's face. It was in that moment that I knew my twenty years sitting at his feet had been justified. Many times, I had asked myself what in hell I was doing spending my life creating fluffy, mindless entertainment for old and young women. It was at that moment, by the giant outdoor Christmas tree, that I realized I had been exactly where I was supposed to be all those years.

After working for PG, I knew I could never work for straight, cut-and-dried publications again. Not only were the tabloids more fun than straight publications, but they paid about five times as much, so I had many things to be thankful for. The Christmas tree experience also confirmed my belief that PG wasn't from this earth. Yes, he died a mortal death like all men, but there remained an indescribable, otherworldly quality to the man which transcended life itself.

PG was the one most influential American journalists in the second half of the twentieth century. More than anyone, he was the prime mover behind the integration of celebrity gossip into mainstream American journalism. He planted and watered the seeds sufficiently that, at the conclusion of the O.J. trial, the mainstream press realized that its audience craved this type of news coverage. As a result, those media outlets that once felt that "gossip"—now called celebrity news—was beneath their journalistic standards, realized that ratings and circulation, and, in turn, their financial bottom line, now depended on it.

Thanks, PG!

In this context, PG changed the face of American journalism for all time.

Today, in an age in which the Internet and digital publishing is slowly but surely sending print publishing to its grave, one will notice that the subjects being presented on the so-called Internet "news" pages are all of the same subjects PG cultivated during the heydays of the *Insider*.

Regarding Ron Jacobs, my colleague in Birmingham who claimed I had reneged on my journalistic principles, he finally won his precious Pulitzer. I'm sure he put it on his mantel and kissed it every morning before going to work. Each to his own, I always say. For my part, I wouldn't swap a single day of working for PG for all of the Pulitzers in the world.

Thanks to PG, I lived a life as a reporter that most journalists would have died for. During my tenure with the *Insider,* I had witnessed the most wonderful, the most horrific, and the most incredible events the world had to offer. Tell me how many reporters with the major metro dailies and all of the millions of minor trade magazines from Paris to Podunk had even seen a six-story-high ball of mud with people, bicycles, cars, and mattresses sticking out of it, or a thousand-pound man or the "moving sidewalks" of Calcutta, or the poor little creature I saw lying on a mechanic's creeper in Altadena, California? How many were ever dispatched to the other side of the earth to investigate one of the great questions of modern history and love one of the most beautiful Asian women God had ever created? How many? One can bet his bottom dollar there were just few.

What a wonderful, magnificent man! Even now, when I remember him in his office seated at his desk surrounded by page layouts, stories, and lead sheets, puffing on a cigarette, my heart soars with gladness. Memories of the statue of Hearst, the bronze "Rosebud" snow sled, the model train track that ran around the periphery of his office; all of this recalls the happiest days of my life. Thankfulness fills the very fabric of my being when I recall that my karma allowed me to know and participate in this man's wonderfully bizarre world. As my editor, he had defined my life. Even as Cortez had defined the life of Bernal Diaz and Gertrude Stein had defined the life of Alice B. Toklas, PG had defined my life. He had made me into what I am today, and I'll always admire, respect, and love him for it.

Clark Gable, the famous Hollywood actor who made millions and rolled around with some of the most beautiful women of his day, once said, "I'm the luckiest son-of-a-bitch that ever lived." No! No! He was dead wrong. The luckiest son of a bitch who ever lived was me, William Donald Johnson, this little ole redneck white boy from North Alabama who lived the greatest life of any reporter who ever put pen to paper, and all because of one thing. I worked for the greatest editor who ever lived, a little Italian man who had enough imagination, intellect, and genius to realize that weird, gossipy, incredible, fluffy, stupid, mindless, woman-centric stories should be reported and published just like "regular" news.

Oh great God! How lucky I've been!

Thanks, PG!

From the very bottom of my heart of hearts, thanks!

The End

Thanks, PG!

Dear Reader:

Once you have finished my book, please consider posting a short review on my book's Amazon page.
The link to the Amazon page for this book is at: http://amzn.to/1Kw8L9S
Reviews make a difference.
It only takes a few words and a few seconds, and it can help enormously.
Without your reviews, my hard work might go unnoticed.
Thanks a million for your support.

The Author

www.ingramcontent.com/pod-product-compliance
Lightning Source LLC
Chambersburg PA
CBHW050633300426
44112CB00012B/1773